Proverbial Spirits

Spiritual messages

*A medium told me to find the Philosopher's stone.
I did just that.*

BY RAY KACZAR

Proverbial Spirits

Spiritual Messages

"A medium told me to find the Philosopher's Stone. I did just that."

By Ray Kaczar

© 2025 Ray Kaczar.

All rights reserved. This book or any portion thereof may not be reproduced or used in any manner whatsoever without the express written permission of the author, except for the use of brief quotations in a book review or academic endeavor.

This is a work of fiction. Names, characters, places, and incidents are either the products of the author's imagination or used in a fictitious manner. Any resemblance to actual persons, living or dead, or actual events is purely coincidental.

Copyright case # 1-15028936341

ISBN : 978-1-970435-08-5

Content

Chapter One

    Biography 5

Chapter Two

    Time to Go to the State Penn! 11

Chapter Three

    Finding Truth 28

Chapter Four

    The Adventures in the Willingness to Rethink Everything You've Been Told! 39

Chapter Five

    Hermes Trismegistus, the Greek God 46

Chapter Six

    Creator God 50

Chapter Seven

    Ariel Archangel 70

Chapter Eight

    The Writings from Seraphim Angel Sandalphon 100

Chapter Nine

Socrates 111

Chapter Ten

Marcus Aurelius Seek Dignity, Not Gold! 116

Chapter Eleven

Metatron 121

Chapter Twelve

John the Baptist 125

Chapter Thirteen

Jophiel, Archangel 127

Chapter Fourteen

Writings from Michael ArchAngel 131

Chapter Fifteen

Miscellaneous Messages from Angels, Ascended Masters, and Others 134

Chapter Sixteen

Quantum Physics? 147

Chapter Seventeen

Carl Jung and My Friendship 162

Chapter One

Biography

An introduction concerning the hardships of my life, which led me to Spiritualism

First things first, concerning me and my life: I am opening up to the truth. Looking back, I would say that 80 percent or more of my life was not worth living for myself. Yet, while I was weak, I was also strong. I spent time in prison, where I had to face my shadow.

Why was I born? Some of you may ask yourselves the same question. As I write this book, I see that I had to become who the Sky Family wanted me to be. Lessons! Archangel Ariel told me best with her writing, *Child's Play*.

Why am I sharing such personal details? Because I no longer want to carry this heavy load that has been dragging behind me for seventy-two years. As Carl Jung taught, we must face our shadow, and this is what I must do. I hope that many of you can resonate with the kind of life you were raised in.

Originally, I intended to make this book entirely about my spiritual communication, which now occupies almost all of my time. If our heart is in the right place, the Spirit will embrace us. Still, I encourage you to find your own understanding of knowing and loving our Creator.

Before I chose to include these personal experiences, I asked my mother and father in Spirit for permission to write about my childhood. They gave me their blessing, and I promised to write as kindly as possible.

What I am about to write, I feel I shouldn't, yet I have to release this to myself somehow. Perhaps others who endured troubled childhoods will understand. At the time, I knew of nothing worse for a five- or six-year-old child to witness. My younger sister was there as well; she seemed to handle it better than I could.

My parents should never have married. All I remember is them fighting, almost daily. The neighbors could hear them, and I was ashamed to walk out the door. As the firstborn, I became my father's target; he often beat me with boards or belts to punish my mother.

One night in our home in Levittown, NY, the violence escalated. My father backed my mother into the kitchen counter with his hands around her throat. His hands were like sledgehammers; though small, he was extremely strong. He choked her violently, I don't know if he realized it or not, how badly he was hurting her, and in desperation, she grabbed a knife from the counter and stabbed him.

I don't think she had time to think about where to do this; it ended up in his heart. My sister and I watched as he fell to the floor. Someone called an ambulance, and he was taken to the hospital. We visited him there; he survived, though he lived the rest of his life with only two arteries feeding his heart. Remarkably, he regained his health and worked harder than most men I've ever met.

Later in life, when we moved to Western NY, he even won an award in the Paul Bunyan Contest at 84 Lumber for driving spikes into a plank. I am not sure, but when he returned from the hospital, my parents tried to get along, but they could not sustain it. I think they wanted to, but it wasn't possible.

My mother also suffered after having part of her thyroid removed. I believe it affected her moods in ways she could not control. Despite everything, I know she loved all of us children.

A rebel was being born, and I became unmanageable by any human on earth. I chose friends who were filled with hatred, just as I was, and I did a fine job of it. One of my friends dreamed of growing up to join the Mafia. The last time I saw him was when he jumped through a third-story window at the Nassau County courthouse, stole a car in the parking lot, and drove to my house. That was the last I ever heard from him. He looked so much like Marlon Brando. The State Police came the next day asking about him, but I told them I had never seen him. I hope you figured things out, Kevin!

Not long after, I ended up in the same courtroom as Kevin. I must have been around ten years old, standing in juvenile court. They incarcerated me at that age, and the children's jail was overcrowded. My cell had only a mattress on the floor, and I cried myself to sleep most nights, asking why I was even alive. I do not remember how long I stayed in the Nassau County Children's Jail; it was probably a month.

My father and mother thought it would help me to attend Catholic catechism classes at St. Bernard's Church. The rebel in me said no. I remember, on Saturday mornings, my father would chase me all over town trying to drag me there. Sometimes he caught me. I recall a nun having us memorize the *Act of Contrition*. I never bothered to learn it. In the following class, many boys did not know it either, and she lined us up to be struck with a yardstick. I was the last in line. When it was my turn, she raised that three-foot ruler to strike me, and I pushed her to the ground. Then I ran out of class and never returned. That was the moment I decided I would never take another beating from any human being on earth again. If anyone wanted a fight with me, I was ready to give them one. Looking back, my sense of self-worth at that time was at net zero.

None of this helped my parents. I grew worse, much worse. I was a rebel with a cause, or so I thought. At eleven years old, my parents sent me to a reform school in Dobbs Ferry, New York. I believe I was there for nearly two years. We lived in cottages that looked pleasant on the outside, but life inside was different.

I am about to share something that only three or four people in my life have ever known. Dobbs Ferry, also known as the Children's Village, was an experience that was not all bad. But it had its share of problematic employees.

We attended an all-boys school there. I had a teacher named Mr. Petrreta, who was a young Italian who thought he was the coolest man alive. He dressed sharply in shiny patent leather shoes and acted as though he were a gift from God. What I remember the most about him is his strange "game." Each boy would place his right foot on a floor tile, grasp another boy's left hand, and then slap the other with his right hand until one gave up. Wonder what I learned from that.

There was also Mr. Brown, my social studies teacher. Once, after I gave a wrong answer, he told me to stand and then struck me in the stomach. I wanted to cry, but did not. To this day, I sometimes wish I could have had him do that when I was older; he would never have dared strike another boy again.

But then there was Bernard. This is the hardest part to let go of, yet I need to release it. I have told almost no one about this. I don't even know his title; he was just always around. We had one cottage, where we did some craft stuff, he took me into a small room, and molested me. He did it again later in another place. I never reported him, out of fear of repercussion.

Not everything at Dobbs Ferry was bad. I had a good friend there, named Gary. He loved the Beach Boys, while Elvis was my idol. His dream was to join the Hells Angels. When I was released, I saw him once more in state prison. He told me he had never joined the Angels but instead had joined their rivals. I can't remember the name, but I know they had a bloody battle with the Angels in Long Island, and many ended up dead. I was about seventeen at that time.

When I was released at about 12 from Dobbs Ferry, I remember my parents wanted to move to Western New York, near my cousins; they thought it would be good for me. In some ways, it was, but no one really understood me. At fourteen, I was living in Sinclairville, NY. Of course, my past followed me. At my new school, the guidance counselor's daughter became my friend, but he did not approve. Soon, people began looking down on me. That dragged me back into my old way of thinking. The rebel had simply moved to a new place, yet it never changed for me. My teenage years were cursed just like my childhood.

At fourteen, my Uncle Bud gave me a job hauling garbage, but I had no license. By the time I was sixteen, he took me to my driving test in a garbage truck, full of garbage. The town police did not bother me; they just wanted their garbage collected.

That job made me strong. It was hard work, and sometimes I had to haul garbage for the towns of Lakewood and Celoron all by myself, while Bud spent a week drunk at the dump. Still, I loved my Uncle Bud. He was like Hercules to me, and I wanted to be tough like him.

He became my idol. He taught me how to drive trucks and operate bulldozers.

I still love him and my Aunt Barb, though they have both passed on. They even bought me an old camper to live in by myself so I could move out of my parents' house. I thought I would experience some positive change in my life, but I was wrong.

Chapter Two

Time to Go to the State Penn!

Here Comes Prison! Bonnie and Clyde. At sixteen years old, I went to see the movie *Bonnie and Clyde* in Jamestown, NY. When I left the theater, I robbed a gas station. A day or so later, I was still thinking about the movie, especially when they were shot down in their car. I guess that's what I desired. Without going into detail, I ended up getting four years in state prison, plus one year waiting for trial.

I begged Sheriff John Bentley to tell the judge to expedite the process. I was in court within a week, and a few weeks later, the Sheriff's Department drove me to Elmira Correctional Facility, also known as Elmira State Prison. The detectives who drove me there never handcuffed me. They were good men. Sheriff Bentley was a wonderful man; the best choice for Sheriff!

For entertainment in the county jail, we fought each other or played cards. By the way, I did get to see Bonnie and Clyde's car in Nevada, the one they were shot to death in, full of bullet holes. I wanted to include that while I can still remember it!

As they walked me through the prison gates, my eyes lit up. *What in the hell did I do to myself?*

Orientation

In orientation, I had to learn the rules. They asked me what I wanted to do for work. I said I wanted to work in the sign shop, where many of the highway signs were made. (The license plates were made in Auburn State Prison. Funny enough, years later, I delivered a load of steel coils there as a truck driver, so they could manufacture the license plates.)

Back in Elmira, my supervisor, Mr. Brant, asked me why I wanted to work in the sign shop. I told him about my grandfather, who was one of the best commercial artists in the world. He had tried teaching me sign painting, hand-lettering, and drawing. Mr. Brant had a kind heart. He gave me brushes, a table of my own, and had me practice lettering every day. He wanted me to succeed, and I gave it my best shot. But I realized I could not become what my grandfather had hoped for.

Inside the Prison were approximately 50 Acres, and they had a giant greenhouse. My desk in the sign shop had a window in front of it, and I could watch the inmates in the greenhouse outside getting fresh air, inside the walls. I spoke with Mr. Brant and told him I didn't think I'd become the artist my grandfather wanted. He agreed. I asked him to transfer me to the greenhouse, located inside the prison walls.

The Farm

A few days later, I had a new boss, Frank, a farmer who lived near the prison. He said, "Follow me." But instead of heading to the greenhouse, we walked through the prison gates where the trucks would make the delivery.' When those big gates opened, I could not believe my eyes; there was a beautiful farm owned by the New York State prison system. I soon discovered that they needed someone who could operate the equipment. I was happy and grateful for this divine timing; it significantly helped me, and I was thankful.

I walked into an oversized garage full of tractors and equipment. Frank gave me a nickname: "Honkey." That was my new name. We became very good friends, if you can understand this. He took me under his wing. We had three farms: one in Big Flats, NY, and two others, including one behind the prison. Our tractor crew only had five or six inmates.

The barn crew had many tasks: we had cows and pigs, we grew grain for the prisons, and we slaughtered the pigs. Then the kitchen crew would butcher them. By the way, we ate very well in prison.

In a short time, Frank made me number one on the tractor crew. This gave me snow duty as well, and I was so grateful. The hacks would crack my cell open in the middle of the night and have me go outside to plow snow all night. To the prison guards, my name was "Pollock." I even had a raise in pay, from twenty-five to fifty cents a day. That was one of the highest wages for inmates. The kitchen staff also made a significant amount of money.

Hard Work and Trust

I had terrible hay fever. Sometimes I could hardly see while cutting hay. Frank felt sorry for me, and he went to the prison infirmary and got me a bunch of pills that helped some. I don't remember what they were, but he gave them to me as needed.

The one farm in Big Flats was on a main road. I watched from the tractor as people walked around the yards, and the pretty girls caught my eye occasionally. I thought about running many times. But Bossman trusted me, and I never betrayed his trust. He taught me about farming, and I loved it!

I was chosen to kill the pigs and gut them. We did this in a small garage in the tractor shop once a week. The barn crew would prepare them after I killed them, and then I would saw them by hand each week down their backbone. It was challenging work; we did maybe six or seven a week. In the winter, we just rebuilt the plows and other equipment.

Frank even let me plant a small garden behind the shop. My neighbor in the cellblock, George, was a mob hitman doing twelve years for killing seven people. Strangely, we got along great. I often brought him fresh produce from my garden. We looked after each other as best we could. As I was coming up for parole, he offered me a job. He said he had a locker in Grand Central Station with all the tools I would need. I thanked him but declined.

One day in the cafeteria (there were two cafeterias because they needed to control us if a riot broke out. The ceiling had gas bombs hanging from it, and there was a gun tower in each one), I told George that deer season was open back home. He looked at me like he wanted to kill me. "How could you kill one of those beautiful animals?" he said. I answered, "I'm not a hunter, but you kill people." He said, "That's different." I quickly changed the subject. In prison, you never ask too much about another man's past

At mealtimes, the inmates liked to brag about who they had killed, I guess so nobody would mess with them. One story I remember was a guy telling his friends how he murdered a diplomat outside the United Nations. Many stories were like that.

Trouble Before Parole

I could go on all day, but it's time to change the subject. One last event I'll share from prison was about my parole hearing. I was soon to appear before the parole board. The farm and the kitchen gangs had very special privileges. At night, we went to the gym to get showers and exercise.

One day after dinner, as I was walking back into my cell to wait until it opened again for showers, an inmate from the barn crew came up behind me and slapped me in the face. His name was Speedy Gonzales, and he was a prizefighter in Sing Sing Prison.

We had boxing too, but I don't think he was part of it. I closed my cell door as we returned from the mess hall. His cell was across from mine in the block. I made a hard decision, knowing I had an excellent chance for parole. I asked George to make sure my cell door got closed because I had a few personal things. I told him I'd be in the Hole for a while and knew I wouldn't get parole.

When the cells cracked open for gym time, he and his friends surrounded me. He had razor blades between his fingers. I begged God to let me land one punch to kill him, because that's what he intended for me. Just then, a hack came slowly walking up the block with his club. I had always feared this guard; he looked a little crazy to me. Yet, he turned out to be one of the good ones. The fight broke up before it started. The hack turned around and left it alone. I felt so blessed.

Later at the gym, Speedy came up to me alone. He said, "You're not like the rest of the white guys. I respect you for standing up to me." From then on, no one bothered me again.

When parole came, I had no problem. I was grateful to Creator God.

Attica: The Riots

When Attica State Prison had the riots because of what Rockefeller was doing, the shit hit the fan in all the prisons of New York. Ours went into complete lockdown. We could only eat one cell block at a time. Each cell had a set of headphones that we could plug into the wall to listen to a television show, a country music channel, or a soul music channel. During the riots, even those were shut down.

The inmates were going nuts. The warden resigned because of the problems we had. I remember one night when an inmate just wanted to stay in his cell. We always walked in a line when going to eat, never knowing if someone was going to shank you in the back. That night, the inmate told the hack, "I want to go back to my cell." They told him no. He got upset, and they clubbed him to death right in front of my cell.

When things returned to normal, I received a letter from the new warden. He told me they were going to send me to a new prison on the Hudson River, Wallkill State Prison. It was known as a better prison, the place where crooked cops usually went. I was honored. Why did he want to do this? I still don't know. I wrote him back, begging not to be sent there. It would have added a couple of hundred more miles for my family to visit, and parole was coming up soon. They let me stay in Elmira.

Looking back, I wonder if it was because I kept my mouth shut about what I had seen. Was my Creator looking out for me? I say yes. It looked like the visions of my future were beginning to come true.

Parole and First Jobs

Parole finally came, and I had to find what we called a "can opener job," something just to get you out of the can. Families could order newspapers to be delivered to inmates, and through one, I found a job on a farm in Westfield, NY.

My family picked me up. I stayed home for one night and then started working on a dairy farm. After a couple of nights living with the farmer's family, I told them I wanted to walk downtown in Westfield to feel some freedom. I was not planning to drink or cause trouble; I just wanted to walk freely, on my own.

The farmer didn't like that. He was a bastard about it. I called my parole officer and told him I was going home. I said if he wanted to violate me and send me back, then just tell me. But he backed me up. That all worked out.

I don't remember what I did after that. I started a landscaping business, and it actually proved to be a successful venture. I had a partner with experience, and for a while it was great, until he and his wife decided they wanted it all. So, I had to find something new again. I always loved trucks.

I needed something to do. Meanwhile, the bars in town were reporting me to the sheriffs, and the sheriffs were reporting me to my parole officer, James Welch. He was from Buffalo, and I was blessed again.

I was hanging out with old friends, getting into fights, and doing things I shouldn't have been doing.

One day, Mr. Welch drove out, told me to get in his car, and we headed to Mayville, where the county jail was located. I didn't say a word, I just listened. Then we made a left turn into the State Maintenance Yard, where he gassed up his car. Man, I sure felt better. I had thought I was going back to the slammer.

Mr. Welch turned out to be one of the best people I had ever met. I told him I wanted to go to truck driving school, that I wanted to drive over the road, Long Distance. He told me I was not allowed to leave the county, but he still managed to get permission for me.

Truck Driving School

I went to the bank and borrowed $1,100 for a school in an old hangar at the Buffalo Airport. I had to travel every day for a few months. I needed gas money, so I robbed a bank. Just kidding. I cut firewood at night by lantern and sold it on weekends. That worked out fine.

The school was basically just an old office. Most of the other students had the Government paying for their tuition. They just sat in the back, talking about women. I became good friends with the instructors, and they went out of their way to help me succeed. One of them even told me, "If I were running a road team, I would choose you to drive with me." That made me feel outstanding.

I passed my test in an old B61 Mack with three stick shifts and no power steering. I was proud of myself for once. It took two hands to shift the gears, and you never stuck your arm through the steering wheel when turning, because it could break your arm. This was around 1973 or 1974.

First Jobs

My first trucking job was with a company that had junk equipment. His name was Nick, but I do not want to share his company name. When I got back, I said, *If this is trucking, I do not want any part of it.*

Then came the big truckers' strike in '74, or maybe it was '75, I can't remember. I was stuck for about a week in Detroit, Michigan. The National Guard was on the bridges. That was a crazy time, but I learned a lot from the drivers at the truck stop.

I couldn't stay with a company that had junk trucks. One day, I stopped on Eagle Street in Fredonia, NY, the home of Fredonia Express. The owner, John DeCillio, looked me over and said, *"I have got someone who left a trailer on the PA Turnpike. Ride down with my city driver. If he tells me, you are okay, you have got a job."*

Fredonia Express had great equipment. The driver I went with was named Oscar. When we got back, he lied through his teeth and told John I was ready to work for the company. Oscar and John are both gone now, but I loved them for the opportunities they gave me.

As time went on, I wanted longer runs. In 1984, I bought my first good used truck and started running coast to coast. I loved it.

Then I broke my ankle while delivering a load from Arizona to Syracuse. I was stuck in a cast for six months. The finance company got tired of waiting and told me they wanted the truck back next month.

The next day, I went to the doctor and demanded that they remove my cast, or I would do it myself right there. They removed it. I welded a bolt to the clutch pedal, cut one of my crutches short, drilled a hole through it, and mounted it to the clutch. I could shift by hand when I needed the clutch. It worked great.

I hired a kid to ride with me since I couldn't climb into the truck or secure loads on my own. We went to Buffalo, where people knew me, and I told them I had just sprained my ankle. Then we headed to Washington State.

After I got unloaded, I found us a room for the night. I soaked in that tub for what seemed like forever. The next day, my company loaded me with steel plates bound for Norfolk, VA, to repair a Navy ship. It paid well. Then my truck blew an engine in Kansas, and I was out of business, stuck with a load that still had to be delivered.

A stranger in a car saw me stranded and took us to an old hotel, the same one used in the Ryan O'Neal movie *Paper Moon*. He was a Bible salesman. It took me forever to climb up the old stairway; the owner, the next day, took me to an airport about an hour away.

A large company called InWay, where I was leased, today has more than 10,000 owner-operators. I knew the vice president very well. He lent me money to get the truck back on the road again. The used engine I had replaced broke the crankshaft, and it went through the engine block. Now I was in Lodi, Ohio, at a truck stop waiting for a ride home. A local junkyard towed the truck off the interstate, handed me a little cash, and that was the end. I was out of business, once more.

I worked for several companies as a company driver. It was all a good experience. A freight agent I knew in Buffalo later went to work for a company called Anderson Trucking Service, or ATS Inc. They had more than 1,200 drivers and owner-operators at the time, around 1985. They took me in, and I got to know the president very well.

The company wanted to start a driver training program, and I was chosen to be one of the first trainers, along with a few others. This was great because I also got paid for the miles the students drove.

I will always be grateful to that company, but eventually, I had to move on.

Somehow, I ended up with seven new trucks again. I always loved hauling oversized freight, and that's what I did for a few years. But the drivers started getting into wrecks, and I lost that business in 1987.

That same year, I was struck by lightning. I went to the hospital and came home. It made me think of that Elvis song, *All Shook Up*. My girlfriend Ann told me it was to become a part of my spirituality.

Somehow, I managed to stay in business, even with outdated equipment. I took on a partner, and together we built a company that grew to nearly 50 trucks before we sold it in 2010. At that point, we were bringing in over a million dollars a month and spending around $1,100 on bills each month. We sold the business, and I took my share of the money and became a farmer.

Farming did not work out; I quickly farmed all the money away. I also had three grain trucks hauling every day. I kept one of them and went solo again. My credit turned to crap again.

I found a leasing company in Tennessee that took a chance on me. I got a nice used truck, and that worked out well. Before long, I was able to purchase additional new trucks. I began working with the largest freight brokerage in the world, C.H. Robinson, and we built a great relationship.

This is a post from Ch Robinson, concerning my first award with them.

Agristar, LLC.

Sometimes you just connect with people.

By C.H. Robinson

Sometimes you just connect with people. It's as simple as having a conversation on the phone, and immediately you know that you just "click" with the other person. That's exactly what happened when Ray Kaczar of Agristar, LLC., called into C.H. Robinson a year and a half ago.

Owner/Operator Carrier of the Year

I'm proud to share that Ray is this year's C.H. Robinson Carrier of the Year in our owner/operator segment. Of our 107,000 contract carriers, we only give out seven awards a year, so it's a pretty big honor to be nominated, much less chosen.

Ray is one of our most dependable owner/operators. One of the best aspects of working with him is his adventurous spirit. No matter how remote a destination is, he accepts the load and trusts us to find another one when the time comes. It can be pretty humbling.

More about Ray: Since 1973, Ray has been in and out of the trucking industry. He's driven trucks for other companies, he's owned his own fleet (48 flatbed trailers strong, I might add), and now he's trying his hand as an owner/operator.

While he'll tell you that he loves the freedom of running his own equipment, he had a bit of a lightbulb moment a few years back. At the time, he was always scoping load boards for his next load. But after hearing Kevin Rutherford talk on Road Dog Radio about broker relationships, he liked the idea of hauling for a broker or two instead of trying to juggle companies individually.

That's when he called C.H. Robinson and never looked back.

Teamwork and technology: A team is the perfect word to describe how Ray and I work together. He wants us to succeed so he can succeed. And vice versa. And that teamwork is made infinitely easier by Ray's willingness to embrace technology.

He uses Navisphere® Carrier on his iPad, and routinely logs into Navisphere on his computer, too. It's really a big advantage for Ray and one of the many reasons he's our Carrier of the Year.

To Ray, I say thank you. Thank you for your dedication to customer service, adaptability in any situation, and thanks for picking up the phone. It's truly a pleasure working with you day in and day out.

And congratulations on being our Carrier of the Year. We're lucky to have you as part of our contract carrier network.

Then came the second award from C.H. Robinson. At that time, I had six trucks, but I was in growth mode and soon worked my way up to 15.

Business Article, 2019

C.H. Robinson Carriers Say Relationships More Valuable Than Technology

By Aaron Huff, May 3, 2019 (updated May 6, 2019)

The 2018 C.H. Robinson Contract Carrier of the Year award winners were announced.

"Digital brokers" are trying to disrupt the $700 billion transportation industry by developing technology to automate freight transactions, such as offering instant "book it now" options to shippers for trucks and carriers for loads.

That line garnered applause from the audience, as did this one from Ray Kaczar, owner of Avalon National in Cassadaga, N.Y., after he accepted his award:

"What you guys have done in my life is beyond amazing, and the journey has just begun," he said. "We are partners in everything. I give thanks to God. I asked Him to lead me to somebody good in this industry, and He sure did."

Before I even added more trucks, I had already been nominated as Contractor of the Year. They were so good to me that they encouraged me to expand, and I did. By 2020, I had worked my way up to 15 brand-new trucks.

Then came the fire. In January 2021, I lost my building to the ground, and I had no insurance. I saved money for the first time and had the cash to build a better one. I thought maybe things were finally turning in my favor.

But then came a downturn in the economy due to the COVID-19 pandemic. Rates dropped overnight. There wasn't enough money to buy fuel, let alone pay my insurance, which cost $25,000 a month.

I told my drivers to bring everything back, and the banks to come and pick up the equipment. They asked if they could leave it for a few months because they were overwhelmed with so many other companies doing the same thing.

This was a shock. How was I supposed to get through it? Before it ended, I was again rewarded for Carrier of the Year. And it was the time I lost everything, again. This time, I was angry. For once, it was not my fault. It was the economy, the pandemic, that fell apart overnight.

Before the end of my trucking life, I suffered a fire that burned my shop to the ground. I had no insurance. For the first time in my life, I had saved enough money to build a new building. But it didn't matter. The economy, and what I was to learn from Spirit, were turning against me. Trucking was over for me. I was now sixty-eight years old.

Battle Scars is a writing Ariel had me put down. I did not want to continue writing it, but it came through anyway. It reads like a poem, and it describes my life.

Battle Scars (2017)

Battle scars of a child's life, they cannot disappear,
things you have seen should have never become so clear,
your eyes have taught your heart deep dismay,
you were so young, you could not ever understand child play!
You have been on an early trial of trying to run away!

Many could never understand this, especially you.
You fought everything that could be good with anger and tossed it all away;
your despair almost brought you to an early death several times.

You loved the ending of the life of Bonnie and Clyde,
the bullet holes you watched in the movie, you were feeling so deep inside,
"Why can't this be me?" you thought.

You were blessed with a grandmother and an aunt who loved you through it all.
Now, from up above, they realize that when they bestowed you with their love,
a miracle occurred!

Later on, outside a town near Memphis, you were in tremendous pain.

You pulled that truck over on the road and asked God to give you more as you said,

"I am sorry." No words were spoken to ask for relief of the pain.

"Please take this life if that is what it takes," you screamed.

We have chosen this body for you to live in on this journey.
We knew the destiny of your growth, it had to be.
For without this, you could not be who you have become.
You could never understand what others must go through.
You could never feel for the hungry who sleep in the woods and streets of the cities.
The people who have made mistakes, now you love to hire them, you adore them!
Realize whose grandmother thanked you because no one would help him with work due to his health issues.

You asked as you began to know us in such a way that we fell in love with your request.
We showed and guided you to where you are today.
There was a time not long ago, you walked near someone with a deadly disease.
We added a noise in your ear that grew louder as you came near him.
As you backed up, the noise went away.

Sometimes you say to us, "I'm crazy, am I hearing things?"
We say to you, why would the mediums edify what you do and think?
This is your proof that we are around you every second of every day.

Your time could be playing and doing what many do every day, but not you!
It is spent talking to us almost all day.
Your requests are to have so much money to build for the cold, lonely, and hungry,
form a community and keep sadness so far away.

You used to shout in the sky to us,
"Give me a small share of what Solomon had; I will show you what I can do beginning today."

You offered us a part of your will; your intent was so strong we had to test you.
You came through. During your tests, people offered to help.
You said, "I will get through this, your thoughts and caring are more than enough. I am OK!"

Look at what has come from the heartaches of the day.
You only ask for one thing. We understand this as you pray.
She knows who you are, and she will arrive one day.

~ Ariel, 2017

Chapter Three

Finding Truth

As a person with a deep desire for truth and justice, about seven years ago, I opened my Bible and asked to be led to a verse that would change my understanding of life. I was surprised by what happened. I closed my eyes, flipped through the pages, and my finger landed on a verse I have never been able to find again. It was in Revelation, written in red print, supposedly the words of Jesus. The verse said that you must have a love for the truth. That was exactly what I needed in my life.

This verse became the perfect reflection of the desires already alive within me. It touched my very psyche. From that moment, my life turned into a journey of spiritual growth and understanding, shaped by sacred virtue and divine knowledge, quite different from the beliefs and practices I had been taught in the past.

But what was to become of me? My desire was to pursue spiritual truth, not just what could be found in books, even the Bible, but to reach for the angelic side of understanding. I longed for the Spirit world to reveal its version of truth directly to me, to answer the questions I carried within. I did seek out the words of others, through places like YouTube, but they never addressed the profound questions of my soul. I realized I needed to speak to the Angels myself.

Many videos on YouTube discuss people's connections with Angels. I cannot speak for them, but I felt a desire to challenge these claims and see where they might lead me. Like many others, I sought a virtuous relationship with God, and I began to realize there was far more to faith than any single religious understanding. I started to see that most religions contained dogma. At the time, I did not fully understand this, but the truth was slowly unfolding. Slowly, I began to understand spiritual presentations that carried a deeper resonance of truth.

Internally, I was starving for a manifestation that would allow me to communicate with the other side. What I did not realize was that the "other side" was within me. I had never been taught that my Spirit, the very force that gave me life, was meant to work in harmony with my human self. Why had no priest or reverend ever taught me this? Instead, all they told me was that if I did not follow their preaching, I would burn in eternal fire. I wondered, *What kind of God am I worshipping?*

Over time, I began to realize that many ancient religions did not preach such ideas; instead, they spoke of different gods and goddesses. The deeper I delved into this, the more I found the God of the Bible resembled a human being, just as most of the gods in other religions were depicted. What was I really beginning to understand? Yahweh, the God of the Bible, declared to Moses: *"There shall be no other gods before me."*

But who was this Yahweh? The God of weather and war? A Levantine human who became the Abrahamic God, and later also the God of Christianity and Islam. They desired a monotheistic God, but I told myself this was not the Creator of truth. Yahweh did not create the Earth or anything else, except, perhaps, deception to some degree. Was he even blasphemous?

Because I now understand, among the hundreds or thousands of gods humanity has claimed to worship throughout history, I chose to call upon the **Creator, the God of Gods.** My choice for the creator speaks to me. I have received several writings from our Mother-Father Creator, which I will share in this book, along with messages from Angels and those we know as Ascended Masters.

Did I immediately begin writing? The answer is no. So much was entering my life at a swift pace. At first, the Angels gently showed me they were ready to make a connection. I permitted them, as I was told must be done, and so I did. At night, they would do simple things, like moving my fingers, to see if I carried any fear. But I loved it. I knew this was the beginning. I became ecstatic as I realized a transformation of my understanding was unfolding. Was I being born again? I believe the answer is yes, I was.

I began seeing numbers, what we call Angel numbers, all the time, and I still do: such as 1111, 444, and others. Then came the visions in the sky. I would see a blue aura around the stars and planets.

At the time, I was driving a semi-truck, and one day in New Mexico, I pulled into a truck stop to take a nap. As soon as I lay down, I looked up and saw two Angels standing in front of me. They stared at me for a few moments and then departed. Immediately afterward, I found myself floating above, looking down, where many Angels were flying beneath me, and I was now in tears of joy! Yet this was far from the last time.

What could happen after seeing such blessings? One night at home, while gazing at the stars, I saw a streak of blue light fall from one star. It looked like a road to Heaven, and the sky above me lit up as countless Angels flew overhead. This time, they appeared in their natural state, as pure energy, and they continue to do so. They have told me it requires a great deal of power for them to appear in human form, and they prefer to remain in their natural state. This was to become my life: conversations with Spirit. From then on, conversations with Spirit became part of my daily life, and I had no idea what lay ahead of me.

Ariel, the Archangel, became my primary liaison, and we have never been parted since. I think of Ariel as female, as I love her feminine side, which makes our friendship feel even more natural to me. She has become my primary teacher, and this has not been an easy task for me; her lessons were tough to understand, yet I learned. There is not a day that passes without us spending hours in conversation. I will share one story.

One night, Ariel asked me to go outside and sit in my chair to watch the night sky. It was cold, and I told her I didn't want to. But she insisted. After going back and forth, I finally gave in and went outside. She told me to sit quietly and not say a word. Sitting quietly, as I gazed at the brilliant night sky, I began speaking to our Creator: I said, "*Father, I love You. I hope I can become what You want me to be.*" At that very moment, a bolt of lightning flashed. I spoke again: "*I surrender my heart to You.*" Another bolt of lightning came. One more time, I said something like: "*I want to serve the purpose You have for me.*" And once again, lightning lit up the sky.

The following night, Ariel asked me to go outside and sit once again. My reply was, "*Now? Right now?*" This time, I simply sat in my chair without saying a word. After about ten minutes, I saw a ball of radiant colors, like a planet, rising from the horizon. It suddenly paused, then disappeared. In that moment, I knew it was God, revealed in the form of divine energy.

Because these manifestations appeared to me, nothing on Earth can ever convince me otherwise: God, the Creator of all, is real. Nothing can shake my understanding of the Creator and His league of Angels, who are willing to share with me. The following chapters will include automatic writings from Spirit, as well as messages from Ascended Masters, beings we call Aliens, and our Holy Sky Family.

The process of my evolution, from the very first day until this day, and continuing beyond, has always carried a deeply rooted concern for understanding within my being, within my *I Am*. In school, I was taught the basics: how to write, how to do some math, and how to memorize a history that had been carefully rearranged to favor the privileged of the Earth.

For much of my life, I wondered: *Have I been blessed or cursed?* For many years, I felt cursed. Yet over the last six or seven years, I have felt deeply blessed. Still, I realize I was born with the same Spirit. I know this because I am still alive. So, what changed? I did. I had to learn everything the hard way. The true understanding of life is not what we are told. What we are told is carefully designed to make us servants of the elite.

They created gods in their own image, human gods, elite beings who demanded worship. I was ensnared in their web of false doctrine until other nations arose, each desiring a god of their own.

Now that I have grown older and can see *my* version of the truth, I ask myself: *What good does it do me?* Perhaps I have only a few years left. My concern now is for the future of humanity. The contentment I find in what I have learned does not bring me much satisfaction, because I see so little change, even as I search throughout history for truth.

I believe God, the Creator, has bestowed upon me a gift, the ability to see with my eyes closed. I do not know where this journey will lead, but I am unwilling to stop. Why do I perceive what is now called quantum physics? Because it is the very energy of life, and within it lies truth.

What I see, hear, and feel is what others call quantum physics. Yet within these concepts is a profound measure of divine truth and energy, especially in what is known as quantum entanglement. I have written extensively about cosmic and earthly frequencies, and I will dedicate an entire chapter to this subject.

It does not matter how smart or uneducated you are. My formal education is almost nothing, yet I know more today because I have a desire to understand the truth. This, I believe, is the greatest blessing of my life. And yet it also hurts me deeply, because so many others do not want to know the truth. They believe they already know it all.

I once walked in those same shoes most of my life, until I was tested. That test made me stronger and a little brighter. Through it, I have been able to see the light in such a way that it carries a quantum essence deep within my soul. My heart cries out for truth and justice to take root on this Earth.

The existence of life on this earth, as it pertains to humanity, is anything but straightforward. Yet it still presents a path to be pursued; a better path, one that could become a superhighway for the road of life. Each of us desires that road of life: beautiful, radiant, connecting us all, just as frequency charges the cells of our bodies with electricity that created life for you and me.

Why don't the teachers understand this? Perhaps they do, but they are afraid, either because they have misled themselves or because they are not permitted to share such perspectives. Why don't churches address these subjects? Instead, they have taught fear; fear of fear itself. Yet fear, though it seems negative, can become a positive force when you face it and understand it. I never thought in my life that I would end up feeling the way I do today, especially over the last few years of my life.

I have taken the fears I once lived with and tried to transform them, learning from each one. They have been deeply rooted within me, and nothing can take that away, nothing! This is because I am willing to ask myself, and to ask the cosmos, about the dwelling place of our Creator, the home where we will reside when we close our eyes for the last time as human beings.

Why was I told I must visit cemeteries and commune with spirits who remain on Earth because they fear a place called Hell? Hell never existed in the oldest religions. It was created to instill fear in your mind and to manipulate your intelligence, so you could be indoctrinated into a world of control. A world where you serve the elite, the super-powerful groups of humanity who understand the truths I am speaking of, yet they will never reveal them to the Earth's population. Why? Because of their greed, their selfishness, and their desire to rule as Kings and Queens.

I cannot understand how politicians are allowed to get away with their actions. Once again, powerful elites manipulate politics, and they are not on the side of you or me. The one thing they fear is a revolt against the source of truth. There is nothing they can do if we all understood what they have been up to for centuries.

You, your spirit, is not new to this Earth. It has been here over and over, as many times as you have chosen to return. So, who were you? What did you learn during your past visits to Earth? What did you know? Most likely, nothing, except how to become a servant of the elite. Humanity should feel ashamed of itself in many ways.

From birth, we are told to grow up, work hard, and then spend the last 10 to 20 years in what we call "retirement." During this time, we visit doctors and are fed synthetic medicines. We work hard, take out loans, and beg for more money to buy bigger homes or fancier cars. But when will we be taught how to live on Earth in a way that reflects the way we should live, as if we were already in the heavens? Instead, we are told to maintain a good credit score to qualify for more favorable terms.

You see, this elitist creation called banking does not apply to the government. Today, we are around 31 trillion in debt. How is it that they maintain a good rating? It's because they print the money and launder it to those who play the control game, those who control you, if you let them. Every president tells us they will balance the budget, but they can't do so if they want to maintain control over the Earth.

All the valuable historical books from the ancients, who knew these truths and were our teachers, have been lost or destroyed, such as the Library of Alexandria and many others. It is said that many of these manuscripts are hidden within the Vatican or other religious institutions. But what I want to focus on right now is our bloodlines. There are certain bloodlines that date back to the beginning of the Earth, which played a role in shaping our evolution. Some of these bloodlines were never meant to be our allies; they were meant to make us their servants. And this still exists today.

Returning to the subject of cemeteries, I tell every spirit that hangs around the Earth plane because of fear that the first thing I ask them is this: *"Do you wonder why you haven't seen an angel come to greet you when you stop breathing as a human?"* They all say yes. Every one of them! I explain that the reason for this is simple: you chose to stay here, of your own free will. The angels tell me they will not violate your decision, whether it's good or bad. It was your choice. But these spirits are loved by the angels, at least, the ones they send to me, and I can bring their attention to this. They can then ask for guidance to be with the rest of their family, who are living in this cosmos now. And often, they do so in my presence. They tell me they see the angels, and a wind usually blows by the grave.

We call it heaven. When I see angels or spirits of other human beings, I mainly perceive them as energy. This is what we are talking about: kinetic energy. This is not the subject I'm focused on this morning as I sit here writing these words.

What I am going to include in my book is not what I originally intended to write. I never thought I would write a book in my life! As for churches, I have visited many different types where various beliefs are preached. Even my understanding of spiritualist churches seems to lack certain elements that I admire. Nothing is perfect, but some of the things we are taught to believe and live by are simply outrageous.

I may feel special for being able to see angels and other spirits, yet it does not make me any more special than anyone else. In many ways, it makes my life harder. Still, sometimes hardship comes when you seek to become a more understanding person who pursues virtue and divinity in the highest form of understanding. We must go through these challenges, as I did when I began my new life of spiritual awareness.

I have been so sick for most of these years, and I have lost the things I once desired, like my business. I am learning that I did not need those things. Life is not about how much you can acquire, nor is it about a person competing with your neighbors or the wealthy. Life is about living naturally and learning to understand nature.

I always thought I had to compete with the Joneses, as the saying goes. Now, I live in a previously owned Amish cabin that was repossessed from its original owner. I have fixed it up, and I am delighted and content with it. I had a lovely home, which was paid for, but it brought me little happiness, or at least very little, after 20 years of living there. What does this mean? It means I have learned that I don't need these things. A nice car is great. A lovely home is excellent. But the conditions of living this life, the things you must concede to, like interest rates, when money is simply printed, put you in debt until the day you die. Where can you find harmony in that? Where can you find divinity? Where is the virtue in serving banks and paying taxes that are not even necessary, since money is printed and not backed by anything of value? Yet, we accept this

Why do we accept this? I wish someone could explain why we allow them to print money and then make us slaves to it. We give them our money, and they charge us a fee for it when we work. We have to pay taxes, why? When we buy a home, we never truly own it after a few years. If you do not pay your taxes, they will take your property from you. Who is anyone to take your property once you have paid for it? The bottom line is that we own nothing on this earth, not even the elite. When they close their eyes, it does not go with them. But what does go with them when they arrive at their new place, which we call heaven? They are questioned. Still, what good does that do us now?

Everything adds up to one thing: it's not their fault, these teachers of deception; it's our fault because we allow others to deceive us. Is this the price we pay for it? The government has stolen all the property of the United States, except maybe Alaska. They killed the original owners, and yet they make us pay with our last breath. Why do we accept this nonsense?

Chapter Four

The Adventures in the Willingness to Rethink Everything You've Been Told!

Division is the most effective way to prevent rebellion and maintain control. Those in power have figured out that people will no longer tolerate such abuse, so now they divide us through political parties and even religion. This division keeps us separated. People might think, *"I've been trying out the Unitarian Universalist Church. I've visited a couple of other churches, and they're good people."* Yet, they remain divided, and I don't understand why. Some of the people who speak and give lectures at these churches are highly intelligent. They invite doctors to speak, yet they constantly criticize the opposing party. The last time I attended one of their services, my girlfriend and I swore we would never go back, driven away by their politics.

I am not saying they shouldn't express their views or that they don't have the right to do so; they absolutely should have that freedom. However, they remain divided and continue to keep themselves separated. They can't see any good in the other party because their own party tells them how they should think, and the same goes for the other side. So, what can we do to see through this and make things more straightforward? We never tell the government "No." Why? What is wrong with us? How did we become so conditioned to follow orders without question, unable to simply say "no"? Are we at the point where it will take an act of God to wake us up and help us see through their methods of controlling humanity? I may not be the brightest star in the sky, but I can certainly see what they are doing. I see it. Our government is more corrupt than the mob, yet we seem content to let them do whatever they want through the election process.

The people who pay the funds to these people running for office don't care who the president is, a Democrat or a Republican; they just need a puppet to do their bidding. You have got the enforcement team, the CIA, and the FBI working behind the scenes as well. Do we have any hope? If we look at it at first glance, the answer might be no.

As someone who can communicate with spirits, they tell me that massive changes are coming. So, we shall see. Right now, in the current political landscape, I can see many changes unfolding. There are numerous chaotic elements within this government, and it is backfiring. It seems that people are waking up, as they're beginning to see the true cost of what both the Republican and Democratic parties are doing.

This book is not meant to be political, but we must understand some of the issues we face. What can you do? What can I do? I know one thing: our frequency, our energy. When we speak to our angelic community, when we speak to our Creator, Father, Mother, God, they will listen to us. They have promised me this. The more energy you invest in correcting the wrongs around you, the more things will improve. So, where do we go from here?

What about your children or grandchildren? The way things are going, it doesn't look good for their future. Why do I even spend the time trying to help others understand? There are many different perspectives in our lives, and the ones you currently understand are not set in stone. There are always other opportunities for change.

You can close your eyes at night and visualize that the angels will hear you. You don't even have to speak the words; they understand what you are thinking. It is the responsibility of every human to make this Earth what it should be. There is hope, and there is always light at the end of the tunnel. It's time to be vigilant and stop letting anyone brainwash us anymore. This is something we must learn. We need to become more aware of our surroundings. We live in an unhappy frequency, and that's our fault, nobody else's, because we have endorsed what others tell us we need to become our best selves, as our future depends on these things.

My Trip to the White House

The House That Became Morganized

March 21st, 2025: We arrived in Washington, D.C., for a four-day birthday celebration for my partner, Ann, the love of my life. She wanted to visit Arlington National Cemetery, which was our primary reason for choosing D.C. as our destination. However, I will focus on my visit to the White House, reflecting on the thoughts I had during our visit this morning, five days later.

I have to say, I felt nothing grand when standing before this iconic home we call the White House! My first realization was that it was no more impressive than when it was first built. But what were its beginnings? The Constitution of the United States, written in 1787 by a group of remarkable individuals, was designed to ensure that all persons residing in the U.S. would be treated as equals. However, 238 years later, it has undergone significant changes, and it is no longer what it once was, not even close.

Our presidency is what I call "Morganized." J.P. Morgan sought a president that Corporate America could control, and the first "puppeteers" were about to take over the United States of America. The first president who was fully under the control of Corporate USA was William McKinley. J.P. Morgan, Andrew Carnegie, John D. Rockefeller, and others financed his campaign. He became the first puppet!

So, I stand here today and realize that we, the people who believe in this system of democracy, have been conditioned to assume our government works for us. But my thoughts, standing so close to this large, imposing White House, are that it has been taken over by scoundrels who are nothing but false advocates of the true meaning of freedom. They claim to serve us, but in reality, they use us to serve their interests. I am afraid this will never change unless more people are willing to be enlightened by the truth.

So, can we ever return to what the founders of our Constitution envisioned? We can, but are we willing to take that crucial first step forward?

Where did the year Before Christ (B.C.) and the year After Christ (A.D.) begin?

Did they need time to write the new addition to the storybook, called the Old and New Testament?

When you read this, ask yourself: Do you see a link between government and religion?

The Bible is an incorporation of writings from many other religions. The Hebrews wanted a God of their own, and it is said that throughout history, there have been at least 50,000 gods or goddesses. The Romans, too, decided they wanted one. At first, they chose to worship Yahweh, the Hebrew god, a man who lived near the Mediterranean Sea.

Then came a man they had to kill because his understanding of truth began to influence others, someone whom the Jews and Roman Pagans could not allow. His name was Yeshua. So, they killed him, just as they did with anyone who did not conform to their laws about whom you must worship.

Around the year 0, before and after Christ, there was a Roman General and Statesman, Julius Caesar. He had statues of himself that said "Christos" on them. Mary, the mother of Yeshua, knew of him; she lived in his time. So, you say there is no "year zero"? That's correct. But why did they create the "Before Christ" and "After Christ" concept? It is because they needed time to separate the man Yeshua from Julius Caesar, the self-proclaimed Christos. So, have they now created a biological fiction? Did they wait many years before they turned Julius into the name "Jesus"?

Why did Yeshua disappear for so long? He longed for Truth and Understanding. He belonged to a group called the Essenes, Jewish people who disagreed with mainstream teachings: Free Thinkers. These years would later be known as the "missing years" of Yeshua's life, his childhood. Many say that, along with the Essenes, he traveled to India to learn about peaceful religions. Spirit tells me this is correct. When he returned, they feared he would reveal everything the Romans and Jews despised: Which is Truth.

So, how and why did the New Testament come into being? Simply because it was the result of a man named Marcion of Sinope, who is often regarded as the inventor of the New Testament. He despised the Old Testament. This began about 140 years after Yeshua was murdered. His doctrine, known as Marcionism, became the foundation for what would later form the New Testament canon. He opposed the scriptures of Judaism. He was a very wealthy man who was a member of early Christianity. But when he pursued his beliefs, his church excommunicated him. Despite this, the story of the New Testament continued, and for many centuries, his church was followed by many.

I don't recall much about him, but Marcion viewed the man he called Jesus as a Gnostic, meaning he didn't fully embrace the Christian dogmas. Much can be found on his history, but I will end this section with one of his quotes: "*O wonder beyond wonders, rapture, power, and amazement, that one can say nothing at all about the gospel, nor even conceive of it, nor compare it with anything.*" Just like Socrates, the government and the church considered him a heretic.

After Marcion, there were 47 more versions of the Bible, yet we must remind ourselves that if you practiced any religion different from what your government or religion demanded, you were deemed a heretic. Despite this, Marcion remains lesser-known as the inventor of the New Testament. So, the last one is the King James Version (Version 48), which incorporated his understanding of the Bible. He was not only a king, but he was also a writer, and his most famous book was *Daemonologie*. He had a fascination with werewolves and, of course, the government. He was a staunch believer in witchcraft. I wonder how the church agreed to this. I do know that some of his cabinet members urged him not to remove certain books from the Bible, and he thanked them by making them slaves. It seems this version was written to appease the Church of England's doctrine, Government-inspired, perhaps?

From the year Zero, it took many years for this Christian understanding to become believable. It took years to write these storybooks and craft them into what they wanted us to recognize as reality. One last question I ask myself just now: *Why did they have to do this 48 times or more?* Some argue it was due to translations, and I can somewhat agree, but not entirely.

6-28-2025

Written by Ray Kaczar with a spiritual understanding of Ariel and other members of the Sky Family

If you are reading this book, then I'm writing to you, and most likely, you will agree with some of it. If you are reading it to see what it's about, you probably wouldn't have gotten this far. Much of the entertainment we engage in is created to distract us from the things happening throughout the world. We only hear one side of the story from the news. I truly wish everyone could talk to the angels and listen to them like I do. I believe anyone could, if it's in your heart to be in the right place. For this Earth to become as it is in Heaven, we must reach as high as we can so that we can proclaim victory for the children who are our future. It is our responsibility.

Chapter Five

Hermes Trismegistus, the Greek God

Prophetic Philosophy

Prophetic philosophy teaches us to desire knowledge of the divine family. The abundance of Christed prisms of natural law is the prime essence of being. To seek truth is to embrace the ability to question all we have been taught, to reach into the unconscious depths of the "I AM," and to reveal oneself. This natural desire to learn cannot be hindered, nor can it be invalidated by deceptive forces that work to inhibit true value.

Opportunity!

Opportunity is not always what it seems. It may appear to be an opportunity, but sometimes it is not. Meditate deeply within the essence of your "I AM." Then you will realize.

~ *Hermes*

Hermes is making me feel good.

About four years ago.

You had not yet begun to open your eyes when I asked you to write a few words. Still, you jumped up, grabbed your computer, and said, *"Sure, let's go."*

I ask because the importance of not having any influence from you is tremendous. You even had to ask me four times if I was truly Hermes!

The ability to understand and become friendly with the other side is a gift. It makes you a medium of great emotional love. You did not take classes. You had no aspirations to become a medium. Even now, you have no desire to give a reading in your church, unless one of us asks you to deliver our thoughts to someone special.

You once asked us to communicate only for guidance in building desires; in other words, never for personal or selfish goals. Your only goal was to serve God. Now you have learned that to serve is to understand God's desire for the earth to become as it is in Heaven.

Your eyes are still not fully adjusted to the light of day, yet you are so willing to do this for me. The council on your floor, number seven, all wish to tell you how much they love this arrangement. That is unusual for us, as it is rare to see teachings and understanding nurture us as deeply as they do with you.

The other day, you said you did not want to be like anyone else. Still, you wished you could sing like E.P.! Ray; you are you. You have matured into the person we always knew you would become.

And now, at times, you even pose a challenge for us, leaving much for us to question, from the top down, throughout the entire council chain.

Sandalphon told you that we would love to see you stand alone, and that is because you can work better with us. You understand this. We know you cannot be alone, and we are doing all we can to become your matchmaking "dating site." We are doing everything to make this reality a natural occurrence. If she chooses otherwise, we are ready to say, *"Yes, Ray, you are not to be alone,"* and we will seek another who desires you just as you would desire her. What you need must be nothing less than what you would call a soulmate.

While you spend so much of your time with us, you also need to experience what heaven on earth has to offer, and we intend to ensure that you do.

I am using less philosophical terminology here because I speak to you as a family member. And, as you know, when I speak in my usual way, it sometimes takes you weeks to figure it out. *Just kidding, but there is some truth in that!*

I devoted my life on earth to words, to the highest understanding of defining them, and then to the ability to express them. You are now beginning to understand the powerful essence of a simple word like *Hate*. For us to see you reach this point is a milestone in our vision of you.

Ray, my advice to you at this early part of the day is simple: *Do not stop being you.* I speak on behalf of your Sky Family when I say that we think of you as being a special kind of special, also.

~ Hermes

Ray Kaczar

April 12, 2025

Transcribing Hermes Trismegistus

Speaking of Truth

Experience withheld, and the value of thought included, will present rhetorical challenges that can only be balanced when one desires actual truth.

What you are told is not necessarily the truth; when you assume it is, shame on you! Your energy plane is living among distorted frequencies. If you accept this, then blessings to you.

But if you desire an eternal destination for truth, you must speak to your soul. Only then can this frequency align with the value that is truly deserved.

~ Hermes

A Morning Reflection

Ray, how are you doing this morning? I have never been asked this question before, while my residence is now in heaven. I am doing well, thank you. My being in spirit is wonderful. I must tell you, this is a wonderful place to be, and we love working with you.

Earth is mentioned in so many ways when we speak with you. Humans make their lives far harder than they need to be. Their desire has become shallow; for they no longer seek wisdom for its true value, or for the knowledge that wisdom itself brings. Instead, they choose to let others, such as governments, decide for them.

We do not live this way in heaven. Heaven is joyous. And no, I am not ready to return, as you must, to earthly life.

~ Hermes

Chapter Six

Creator God

Our Creator tells me I am to write a book in the year 2019. Now, in 2025, I am collecting my automatic writings for this purpose.

Prelude for Evolution and the Existence of Truth

Ray, you will eventually write a book, and others will help; I will bring them to you. It is time for all who sleep in blindness to have the chance for enlightenment to arrive.

You asked me this question: *Are there any other planets that have life forms and live in harmony, the way you desire life for life to live?*

My answer is yes! They understand who they are; very few of you on Earth understand this.

~Creator God~

About 2019

The Plight of Humanity

Understanding the plight of humanity is straightforward. I have created a map for your destiny to shine bright like the sun. You must choose: either the laws of your Creator, or the laws that man has designed for you. Choose one!

Ask me in your heart what this means, and I will reveal it to you.

~Creator~

Conscious Spiritual Development

Incorporating a self-earned desire to exist in a world of so much misunderstanding creates gravitational frequencies that prevent one from going beyond what others desire.

To be brave and take a giant leap forward can spark the rebirth of who your essence was meant to be.

Ask yourself: *Are you living within your truth, or do you live according to what others tell you is your only option, what you only feel is the truth?*

~Creator~

Your Heart Is Full of Hurt and Anger

Raymondson, your heart is full of hurt and anger. You take on the hurt of the Earth through your heart's desires. Your understanding of our desires is a gift we knew we could share with you over the last several years of your life.

I have made decisions with the entire Team you call your Sky Family. Change is in the air, and that phrase is becoming a literal truth. Humanity is beginning to see this with their eyes; eventually, their hearts will speak to their brains. If not, they will feel it through what they experience. I will not elaborate further on that.

Traditionally, the cycles of life have been carried forward through the return of humanity by the gift of reincarnation. Yes, the incarnations are those who have been chosen to help. None are forced to accept. As I speak with you, you wonder: *What happened that people still don't get it?*

It is as if they forget their assignments. In spirit, they are not compelled to return with specific tasks when reincarnated; their free will remains intact. The few incarnations who choose to serve take on roles for many reasons. Each may have different assignments, yet their free will remains intact.

We, your Sky Family, are heartbroken that even most religious people cannot see beyond what they are told to believe. As I mentioned earlier, change is in the air.

Our family did not create this vast, beautiful environment so it would dwell in despair. Yet with each passing moment, it worsens. Still, it must happen naturally; we force nothing on anyone.

We have been patient, but the changes we see are not what they should be. These are shaped by the teachers and controllers of your environment. So, we are changing the frequency of the environment. Each human should desire this, or live with the results of their choice.

I am dismayed to see so many accept unnatural laws and live by them. When the skies become angry, understanding will bring an awakening for many to rethink.

~Creator~

Channeled by Ray Kaczar

08/07/2025

Our Creator is speaking to me on July 4, 2025

Raymondson, your deep interest in the past has become the doorway to the beginning, concerning the Earth where you have resided. I hold the highest respect for your desires, and I am genuinely sorry they were not fulfilled as you thought they would be. There was nothing wrong with them; I knew this from the start. I wanted you to experience them. Yet, as patient as I am, you have grown older, and it has taken you longer than our family expected. However, you have now reached that point. It is time for us to move forward.

There has been so much chaos, misunderstanding, and misteaching of our children throughout the millennia. We will dive into why this is happening. This will reveal the truth of why I retain the rules that I do. You are always asking me to break a rule, to make this Earth just for all. My intention during the early days of Earth was to see your planet evolve as many others have throughout the solar system, or the universe, as you understand it. But this did not happen.

This is not the first time you have heard the story of your family, the Anunnaki. As you know, they were born as the Elohim.

Your questions to me, and to Ariel tonight, have ignited a spark deep within my thoughts; looking back from the beginning to where we are today upon your Earth. There are many stories concerning our family. I will share more with you in a series, so you shall not forget.

Ariel has asked you many times, or at least placed the thought within your mind: *Do you want to know who you were in your previous lives on Earth?*

You said, *No, not really; I can hardly live this life.* Yet now and then, the past reaches out to you. Tonight, with the questions you asked Ariel, I was listening. When you asked, *Am I?* and Ariel answered, *Yes,* I saw the confusion on your face. I saw all your thoughts racing through your mind at once.

In that moment, I felt the desire to bring forth the truth once again, concerning humanity, and concerning you.

The Elohim family is who we are. We are the first source. Our family is vast.

Many of us are what you call angels. *Angel* is a good word with us; it sounds pleasant and creates a gentle frequency, something much of your language often distorts.

For a purpose, the beginning was a process of evolution, an expansion of growth across what you understand as millions of years. Our family grew, and our lineage gave rise to other lineages that carried much of our essence. Now we have new families, each with its own desires, which we welcomed as family. Planets were built as places where people could live, different from Earth, with unique environments. Not all were equal; not even in the air to breathe. The universes, or galaxies as you call them, are never-ending; each has its own frequency.

As our family expanded, we longed to create new life. We progressed and eventually built planet Earth. This took many years. The seeds of life were planted, and humanity began to exist. But Earth needed extra help from above. By this time, life throughout the cosmos had grown, and the Anunnaki gathered their offspring. They came to Earth to help it become what it was meant to be. Independence and free will became central to humanity's evolution.

This created events as time moved forward. Those you call aliens, I ask you to call the Anunnaki; your family of the Elohim, direct blood.

So now your Earth was blending genetics until the first humans appeared. Many others contributed their genetics as the Anunnaki grew, and new families became abundant. Humanity now carries mixed blood. And your Earth is about to enter a serious time.

At first came what you call Lemuria. These beings looked nothing like humans today, but they were of your family. They felt a freedom that was entirely new, living as humans upon their land. Over time, they forgot who they were, their roots. This was acceptable because it was part of evolution. That was the goal. This is where it began.

Understanding the beginning is a crucial part of understanding anything at all, Raymondson. In recent years, you have studied many lessons concerning mythological gods and goddesses. Through these lessons, you learned truth; not from words, but through direct experience. Looking back, you felt pain, but it gave you the ability to see forward more clearly than you ever thought possible. Your willingness had to be proven, and it was.

The visions you have seen in these past nights are crucial to your understanding of who you have been, and who you have always been. You are the same essence, only in a new body; a new formation of frequency, born as a human, to represent our understanding and our truth.

Let us return to the beginning. Life arose on a continent that no longer exists. Humanity has tried to erase the story, but somehow it continues, and the story has grown throughout time. Long ago, the first of the first came to your Earth. They gave birth to new humanity, new families, and new lineages. These became the offspring of our Anunnaki tribe.

Your deep desire to understand who I am remains. The Creator you call me? I am a chosen one among those you call angels. This is because I was the first to become the source.

You wonder: *Did the other angels come after me?* They came with me, as if in an instant, like the snap of a finger. Was I first? Think of it as the first drop of rain striking the ground. Yes, the other drops followed, falling almost at the same time.

And so, we became the first form of life. Before us, there was only what you might think of as an abyss.

Father, Creator, I have a question for you: *What was with the abyss, and then you came along with the angels, the Elohim?*

Raymondson, the abyss contains frequency. That frequency carries the ability to communicate, but it only recognizes what you call love. We are all, humanity, beings from other planets, and you, products of this frequency. We are the first representatives, which brings great responsibility.

On your Earth, religions have formed throughout time. Many of those you consider gods or goddesses were tested by their people in their regions. Different nations sought to proclaim their gods and goddesses, which led to inquisitions across many lands. The way to enforce these beliefs was often through war.

Free will enabled them to act, and it led them back to the first continent. Yet it became unmanageable; their egos could not live in harmony.

Our little conversation will continue in time. This will give you plenty of opportunity to think and to ask us more questions. You are truly the one we want to give answers to.

Transcribing God — July 4, 2025

Creator, why do you let wars continue?

Dear Creator, God, I have a question for you. So many ask: What kind of God would allow this Earth to continue with wars, murders, and corrupt governments for centuries?

Please explain this to me.

Creator:

I would be happy to. The iniquities of humanity are a disgrace to your Earth. Their false stories are the reason humanity remains ignorant of the true nature of the Creator Source: the frequency of light.

This light is not like a lightbulb that you switch on; it is the truth, and it can be understood and obtained. But if you are not willing to delve deeper into your subconscious, you will accept only what you are told, and you will live with the consequences of that so-called truth.

True light is hard to find in your world today because of the deceptive practices of those who are clever in hiding it. But remember this: I know their names.

Automatic transcription from the Creator

In the beginning, we became the Elohim.

And the Earth began its birth.

When the Earth was formed, her skin was rough, her winds were brutal, and humanity could not yet evolve. The alchemy was lacking the love of the essence of herself.

This became step one for me. My creativity for eternal life always existed; we, at this point, had not yet brought Spirit to live through the existence of who you are.

We made Earth brilliant for humanity to be created; my children, who would be happy and live in harmony with the blessings that were important for the joy of life!

Everything for sustainability was here; you were given the knowledge that was so powerful. Then, understanding among yourselves emerged: you were brilliant throughout the generations. However, you forgot where it came from.

Some men understood this, and they thought they were gods; some consider themselves the same today. My gift of letting you make decisions in your own life is what you call free will.

Your gift, this blessed honor to be a free thinker, has been hindered by clever abilities to control your knowledge base and make you feel you need to be on your knees begging me to help you!

If the truth were ever told, it would be mine right now! Throughout the history of linear time, humanity has been a failure.

I created all of you to understand the depth within your soul, to know who you are. Until you realize natural divinity and understand that this will not come from the dictatorship of man and the selfishness they seek, you will all continue as you have through the ages.

You all can make your home in common unity! For I would never tell my children they should breathe the dogma of fear and hellfire. If there ever were such a thing, I would say many of you are creating similar punishment!

Natural law is hidden from most of you. I would like to see it return. Your hearts must understand that change is needed and that your rules for life engagement will not coincide with mine.

Hatred is your strongest crime; ignorance follows. Your heart, beautiful as a rose in full bloom, should have understanding for growth! My love will never abandon you; you do this to yourselves!

I am asking these words to be written because I am in tears watching my children run around the earth, killing each other and being proud of it, all because the leadership in your nation tells you to. What happened to *Thou shalt not kill*?

Only all of you can change this earth to become as I have designed it; it is your job! The key to life is to have a desire to love your God and then ask to receive the truth for understanding. We are waiting for your heart to call upon us!

~Creator~

There Is No God but God

Hello, Ray, and this delightful community of Spiritualism. I must confess; even I get tears in my eyes when Ray sings the song, "There is no God but God!"

I never stop pouring my love upon all of you. I want you to know: the hardships in life are man-made. Your free will gives you the opportunity to decide whom you will follow. I allow this.

Men hide my truth, yet all of you are as divine as any of the angels, and as divine as myself. What will it take for you to show me the love for what we created for you?

Until you decide to become and understand what your purpose is, hardship will always remain upon your Earth. I will never interfere with your gift of free will.

Let me tell you that your task is to desire Earth to become as it is in Heaven.

Blessings!

~Creator God~

The Clover Seed and Heaven on Earth

Ray's Spiritualist focus should aim to teach the essence of showing the afterlife as a guide to Heaven. This is an important aspect for growth, as you have shown in your words to us.

You asked: *How can I be of help?*

I just told you. Like the single seed of a clover, it grows underground and propagates into millions of plants. This is the beginning of creating Heaven on Earth.

If a single seed of clover can do this, so can you.

~Creator God~

Masculine and Feminine in Creation

When I Created Life,

Everything was formed with both masculine and feminine sides. In time, this form of life on Earth will grow into an androgynous state of being.

This is because, as we are in Spirit, Ray calls me Mama, yet he also speaks to me as Father; for we are one. It is difficult for many to understand, as they are not ready to see with their eyes closed. Yet many can.

~Creator~

The Birth of Earth as Mother

When she was created,

She was in a full storm. As her time began to unfold, she grew in her ability to provide and to give for what was to come. Her love carried the power to create, and so it happened.

Her creations gave way to understanding, and she taught everything how to create as she did. May I ask you, are you one of those creators?

This lady's name is Earth.

~Creator~

A Conversation on Love and Companionship

Early Morning Talk with Mother Gaia, concerning your desire for a life mate, Ray, your concerns are not unnoticed. Your request is a challenging one to fulfill, due to your inner needs.

Your last friend was a wonderful being, but you left because she did not share in your spiritual essence. As Ariel has told you, this is a tall order to fill. Keep the desire, and search deep within your *I Am*, for she exists.

Your spirits will complete the miracle of this very natural yearning. Not many are willing to go without. But you are. You will know her by the sweetness she carries deep within.

~Creator~

The Scale of Love

The scale of love is weighed by the amount you hold, and this is a Natural distribution. Some may have to wait longer for it, while others will grow into their inevitable paths.

~Creator~

Ray's Heart and Divine Trust

Ray, I tell you, your heart is reaching deep into your past. You are confused, yet you are willing to trust and to understand all that we are doing.

You asked for this, and I knew it was more than you expected. But you can handle it. We love you. We are your family in the sky.

~Creator~

Love Above Karma

Karma and love are not a very good recipe. The alchemy does not blend well. So, stay focused on love, and let karma take care of itself. For the true understanding of karma is that it stirs within your consciousness. Karma knows its own path, and love travels in another direction.

To worry about karma does not hold value. Yet a deep desire and understanding of love is invaluable. Desire it. Become it.

~Mother Gaia~

Free Will, Responsibility, and Human Choice

You have asked me if it would be better to separate the bad or compromised spirits living within humanity. I have given you all the freedom to choose.

If I were to do this for you, then perhaps you would have submitted to me, just as you submit to the leadership of mankind. Yet all of you are sons and daughters of God. Would an honorable Mother or Father lead their children into darkness?

Be the light you are blessed with.

Ray asked me if the dark, compromised spirits can be separated. I say this: you, as humans, are responsible. You must depend upon your diligence and independence, and be free thinkers. Choosing the words of the wealthy may make some of you lazy in thought.

If you want freedom, demand it. If your choice is to live like a droid, you are free to shape that variety of life. But please consider the offspring of your family's future.

I hear people say, *Dear God, please help me*. And I answer: *I did. You were born with a mind designed to think freely*. Many let it grow stale, by their own choice.

As the Mother of Mothers, I gave you free will. Your task is to make Earth an environment of freedom, where you look after one another.

The birds, the ants, and the entire animal kingdom serve humanity in perfect harmony. They were created to sustain and maintain life support for you.

The air and water were never meant to make you sick with any disease. I did not create sickness. What you call sin did not create sickness. Humanity has allowed sickness to evolve through the tampering of alchemy, believing that some of you could do better than your Holy Family.

That is all the Divine can do for you. I have given you simple, natural laws to choose from. If you seek, you will find. If you do not, you will continue to become what you are because you let others convince you that they know more than you.

Your choices, allowing the world to indoctrinate you, are paying you back for what you have sown. But free will and free thinking can change everything, at great speed. Love can change everything.

Your Holy Family, here and all around you, is ready to bring change. Your task is to understand what is needed, and then ask, as Ray does. This is why we spend so much time with him. He carries a clear vision of desire, and shares in our own desire as well.

Many believe that half of you are wrong and half are right. But I tell you this: all of you are wrong if you do not understand *why* it is wrong. Until you do, you cannot find the change you seek.

Knowledge from many brilliant philosophers is available now. I appreciate the words of wisdom Hermes first shared with Ray in his initial automatic writings. He said: *When you desire to know us: your Holy Family, within your I Am, then nothing can hinder your progress in creating with the understanding of truth.*

I am saddened that humanity has come to depend on clever, wealthy, self-serving people to tell you how to live and think; when I gave you the ability to think, and to ask us to help you choose.

I have been with Ray this morning. He is very tired, yet he willingly gives his essence of love to me, and offers his will for the mass understanding of truth to shine.

Angelic Acupuncture

A holy, divine healing; narrated to the angels and dispersed through the love of Sandalphon, the Seraphim who sits with God at the Divine Council's table.

I am going to display this gift to someone in this group who can feel it most strongly. Your yearning to understand and to share love has touched our hearts.

Your love is pure, and we are about to touch your life with an abundance of what you are deserving.

~Creator~

I Feel Like Moses Writing the Commandments Right Now!

OUR CREATOR IS TELLING ME TO WRITE THIS AT 3 IN THE MORNING.

The time of the Great Awakening has now begun. Your Holy Family sees that it is time for the arrival of new, life-changing methods that will create greatness among our children on the Earth plane.

When you recognize that we exist and that we provide you with the laws we have created for your life, rather than the deceptive teachings and manipulations of mankind, you will have become a pioneer in this new awakening.

For those who can understand this, your blessings are already beginning to sprout. First, you must know who your Holy Family is. You must understand the truth of our existence, and not the fearful talk you have been taught all your mortal lives.

Do not be caught up in the rhetoric of liars and clever deceivers. This includes many religions and political forces designed to manipulate and control you. For I, your Mother Gaia, have initiated the greatest change mankind has ever seen.

Expansion of consciousness is coming to those who seek us. You will be among the first to begin shaping Earth into what we desire it to become. Humanity has been sleeping in mortality for too long. This means many are like the living dead. You have listened to mankind's teachings of fear for so long that you have been taught to fear us.

But if you can see beyond the deceptive truths, your blessings will arrive in an instant. We ask that you desire the pure love of life's truth in your heart. Then your soul will begin to understand the nourishment it needs, and God will bless this upon you.

~Creator~

Yeshua and the True Spiritualists

Yeshua and his group were the true spiritualists. They feared nothing concerning natural law, not even sickness. They could cure sickness because they were true to their hearts.

Those who fear sickness, yet claim to be healers, are frauds. Let them be who they are, and you: be yourself.

~Creator~

Tough Love from the Mother Creator

Mother Creator, our feminine side, tells me what we should consider!

Automatic writing again, Ray. I thank you for your heartfelt concern about what is happening across the Earth. You ask me to consider your thoughts, and I do this, Ray. We all think of these things.

I will give a brief overview of humanity and the strife it *serves*. That is right; *serve!*

Thousands of years ago, I gave you the ability to live without strife, sickness, or hunger. Yet your spiritual past has led you astray. Many believed that as you evolved, you became wise enough to figure it out on your own. Then others discovered that if someone else could do their work, they could control and enslave. They taught you less, and they made you servants of men. And now, you are right back in this cycle.

I have seen blind and deaf men since birth understand truth better than most of you. You fall to your knees and beg for help, but I gave you that help when your essence was first birthed.

You have let me down. Now you worship governments and schools that indoctrinate corporate control. You have sown this, and now you reap it. Cavemen knew how to live better than many of you. Animals understand love better than many of you.

I, Mother God, am angry that my children choose the rules and indoctrination of men over the divine gifts I have given you. I shout to you now: the way you think will only bring more distress and sickness. Soon you will become living droids, and this is of your own making.

I love you all so much, but this time, it comes with tough love.

You want me to show you paradise? It will only come from the power and love that created you. Nowhere in any of the universes will you find this. I, your Mother Creator, made you. Yet many of you refuse to know me.

I have enough love to let you figure it out on your own. But I am not impressed.

Call upon me from deep within your heart, from the depths of your inner self. I will send angels to bring you home, to teach you everything there is to understand about the love of truth.

~Creator~

First Life

The light of life!

Fractal rays of cosmic light are an eternal part of existence, in and of everything. This is pre-creation, when like-minded species of light organize, they begin to procreate. And with procreation, subatomic structures begin to atomize, and existence itself takes form. Thus, the representation of all matter is highlighted.

Its origins can be considered ordained spectrums of common unification, which then grow into internal understanding. From birth, the brain develops this capacity. It must learn its abilities.

Humanity is a combination of all the above. Your brain is a gift of knowledge, a sacred union with your heart. The heart guides the brain to understand that your internal spirit is the true beginning of your entity.

Each and every one of you is blessed with the gift of independent existence, spawned from the Creator Seed of Light.

Creator Source

Dear Creator, please hear my plea.

Please send me the woman you desire for me!

The Answer

Mother-Father God, tonight I realize, more than ever, that I am your son. Our angels have bestowed Holy Grace upon me from the sky, allowing me to see this with my own eyes.

Ray, you make me proud when you pray to Our Father who art in Heaven. Thy Kingdom come, and you will serve to see it done on Earth as it is in Heaven.

Get ready to see what we shall do together. We will bestow a Queen of Avalon upon you soon. Your will shall become the foundation for Earth to rise into its true design.

We are ready for change. It must come from all of you who desire it, and it has already begun. And when it is truly desired, Ray, as Hermes has told you, nothing will be allowed to hinder it. Never.

~Creator~

Chapter Seven

Ariel Archangel

Voluptuous Mary Magdalene!

Mary Magdalene, voluptuous as she was, was never a whore. Yeshua and she had two children. They lived in a time when the matriarchy, meaning women made great decisions, was being torn apart by the patriarchy: "Listen to what the men say, listen to what the men write, or else." The Roman Empire would never have allowed a woman to have the kind of respect that, from their perspective, only a man deserved.

I declare this family has a great deal of lineage walking the Earth in your times. We are tired of the persistent falsehoods that have been perpetuated for over 2,000 years. You still believe what your governments tell you. I'm telling you: you have very closed minds if you are not willing to change your thoughts, as Yeshua did in his own time.

He was crucified while Mary watched him die, pregnant with his daughter, Sarah. The religion you chose contained the art of patriarchy throughout its church. You consider Catholicism to be the first choice; other religions became known as Christian spinoffs. They added their dogmas and eradicated the parts of the Christian faith they did not like.

If you think Yeshua would have said, *"Forgive them, for they don't know what they are doing,"* while watching the woman of his life pregnant with his child, knowing he would never hold her again as a human, you are mistaken.

— *Ariel Archangel*

Mary Magdalene Telling Me to Get a Shower, Relax, and Write!

Feeling down in the dumps today, business is more than a challenge, and so are my personal desires. I reached the point where I told myself, *"I see no reason to even go to church tomorrow!"*

Ariel told me, *"You're going to church."* I replied, *"I know!"* At 11:30 tonight, Ariel said, *"Go outside and sit for a minute, in a chair."* I knew from past experiences not to question her.

Within a minute, I looked up into the sky and saw another spirit approaching me. I asked, *"Are you Mary?"* and she replied, *"Yes."* Somehow, I knew it was her. She told me to take a shower and asked me to write down her thoughts.

So here we go, Ray. I am Mary Magdalene. I came to visit you tonight because I feel your heart crying. We are so close through the centuries that I think and share in your tears. In this life, you are only beginning to understand how deeply we have been connected— forever and ever.

You, Ariel, and I are related in a special spiritual hierarchy that spans both the past and the future. Within your human body, you have a profound desire to know your Holy family and to serve Father

God. We are proud of your endeavors in seeking human enlightenment for mankind.

It is we who strive for affection, yet we cannot meet the requirements of creating the development of polarity so that creation may progress. If you are unhappy and want to love someone, why would you wait? Why would you pass up heartfelt desire?

Your life deserves all that you want to give in return, and for your desire to receive affection as well. Enjoy what you have while you still have it.

~Ariel~

Earth's destiny is an absolute for creating change. Your spirit has visited Earth many times in different vessels. Realize this, and you can begin to understand the reason why you return. This understanding is a bright way to rethink much, and it can make for a better human experience for you and for all others, including all forms of life.

Your Creator God allowed you to evolve for a reason called growth. Realize that you are sons and daughters of Mother-Father God, and try to follow in the desires of their creation. As Ray knows, they are saddened that so many are selfish with great amounts of greed, desire change, and ask for help from any of us. It shall happen, and Father-Mother God will be joyful to see that you wish to cherish this beautiful planet they created just for you. Natural law is **key** to its progress.

~Ariel~

Believe in us, and your truth will become the essence of your daily tasks. It has an influence that may reveal to you what your eyes have been closed to all your life.

We can be considered precious gifts. We do not charge for this; we, the angelic helpers, are free.

~Ariel~

We are monitoring the Earth, and all that is happening, particularly with the unrest in governments. Free will reigns on Earth for everyone. Your will can make a change. Just desire what you feel is needed, with no hate.

~Ariel~

I asked Spirit: *"Is America going to fall by the wayside?"*

"Yes, Ray, your citizens allow criminals to preside over their lives. If you were Creator, would you allow blessings upon people who are too blind to see and too afraid to act?"

~Ariel~

Hello friends, I am Ariel.

I want to extend a good evening to all of you. The Earth is becoming very angry with the diverse tactics used by your governments. There comes a time when you, as an individual, must ask: *"What can we do to make great change?"*

The easiest way to change is with love and respect for your self-worth. Value in this becomes a positive aspect of you. You then reciprocate your value back to the universe, and your energy becomes like that of light. Light has so much value that the dark cannot hide in its deceptive highlights of forced corruption.

As a result, all things that give in to this dark, man-made environment cannot even suspect they shall survive. Desire change, and it shall be done. Just as it is in Heaven, so shall it be upon your Earth that Heaven created.

~Ariel~

Love Is in the Air! Called Truth!

Early in fact, in the beginning, humanity lived with a natural understanding. Then came those who saw the potential for misusing this insightful natural ability to change the version of it.

It became a selfish law, and most of you willingly accepted this change. Now, you can see the manner of control they possess over your humanity.

~Ariel~

Our Love for Your Soul Revelation

Think of the soul as the aura of the heart. The spirit brings life to the heart. The spirit has chosen to come from heaven and place life into a vessel, the human body.

When the spirit enters the vessel, breath begins. When the spirit departs, the soul remains with the body, and the spirit returns for another journey to heaven until it decides to come again.

~Ariel~

I asked Ariel: *"What is going to happen to the ordinary citizen soon?"*

He replied:

"I will speak to you concerning the deceptive forces that are in great abundance. These humans speak with tongues that can't even tell the truth to themselves anymore. Yet on the other hand, the

ordinary people, by their lies, when it becomes so desperate for humanity, more wars shall arrive.

This will be their excuse. These deceivers will still live comfortably. They always have, and they always will, until the ordinary people wake up. This is what it may take to wake people up."

Ariel, an Archangel, told me, "Let us write something while you rest for a little while."

Blessing became reality this past Sunday for you. I watched and smiled as you spent precious time with so many wonderful people at Lily Dale. At church, you helped a wife who had recently lost her husband. Your friends waited for you to join them for lunch after your council meeting.

You shared precious moments with wonderful people at lunch, and after that, your happiness continued until the Stars told you it was midnight. Around midnight, an angelic manifestation appeared in the sky to your friend. We feel very blessed to be in the sky and see so many people sharing laughs and smiles.

~Ariel~

That night, I asked Ariel, an Archangel: "Why do animals have to eat each other?"

This was his short reply:

"God knows that life is life; this means that one must feed upon another. So, I say, why don't all of us eat plants? The answer is this: humans eat animals, but not many animals get to eat humans. The diversity breaks down to the smallest insects, and the waste from all life creates life for plant life to grow. Plant life, in return, gives us oxygen.

It may sound gruesome, yet it works well. Life is balanced by natural law, and the balance is so perfect that one should understand this as a gift to the human species. Humans should return to life with the purest love for one another. Because they do not, we have sickness, suffering, greed, selfishness, and so on—all acts of unnatural law."

~Angel Ariel~

Great Morning from Ariel

Today is a great time to understand your tears. Ray calls tears *Holy Water*, and I agree. Tears of love and of sorrow are created by the feelings in your heart, either joy or sorrow. Life for most goes on with joy and sadness for many. Seek the pleasure, for it is always there to find.

Even we cannot, like magic, simply say, *"Be happy."* So, what can we do, you may ask? Your desires can be taken into account by us. Yes, we can help with them.

Understand that the principles in the church Ray attends say you are responsible for your happiness or unhappiness. This is part of understanding natural law. All of you can grow in this understanding if need be.

~Ariel~

Living in Joy or Sadness

The state of a person living in joy or sadness depends upon the desire to understand a current situation. You can either accept it or return it, just as you would with something purchased from a store. Not all sadness started as sadness; it often started from what was once desired as love, or at least the hope of it.

One should understand that desires manifest over time, and they may eventually become undesired as people change. The ability to truly enjoy love must come from like-minded souls; otherwise, it simply does not work. A change of habit goes a long way toward allowing happiness to arrive. Seek, and you shall find. Ignore, and you shall remain where you are, just be sure.

~Ariel~

Our Mother-Father Who Art in Heaven and Throughout the Universes of Creation

I was asked by you, Ray, tonight: *"So many say the God of your understanding, the energy of the Universal, and on and on. Ariel, what does God prefer?"*

My reply is: *All is good.* Yet, when you call God *Mother, Mama,* and *Father,* you acknowledge the masculine and feminine energy of the Holy Spirit. Mother loves it when you call her by this title. You can do this by understanding her and asking her what you can do to make her proud.

All of us on this side of the spiritual spectrum have a fascinating relationship with you. Ray, the one thing you have proven is your faith in Natural Spiritual Holy Law. Your understanding of Domestic Law cannot, and never will, blend with what is Holy.

Look at your pain in the last few months, when you were hurting so badly. Many of your friends asked you to go to a doctor and seek medical treatment. Your reply was: *"The Holy Sky Family told me no! We are your healers."*

As your pain became unbearable, you asked for relief from us, and it was instant every time. We taught you that the healing process is natural and Holy, as it was in the beginning—this is how it was meant to be.

We walked you through this event, and some of your spiritual friends who care for you offered love. The combination of both was knowledge of what is supposed to exist on your planet. Your healing is now almost complete, and you tell us, "Thank you." You felt an Angel working on your leg, and you told her, "Thank you, I love you!"

Your gifts from us are deserved. You would be willing to do anything we ask of you, even during your trials of life. I am saying this because we want the whole Earth to know that this is what we want for every human. We always have.

Every human should ask us not to forgive them, but to ask for understanding of the Divine, both in Heaven and within themselves. You must absolve your wrongdoings, and this includes prioritizing domestic law over the Kingdom of God.

~ Blessings Arch Angel Ariel~

What Is a Soul Mate?

You ask me, Ray. A much better word for this is *Spirit Mate!*

The spirit that gives you life, or gives anyone life, must be in harmony with the spirit that resides in the mortal who is trying to build a permanent relationship.

For the rest of life's relationships, one person may get along with another, but do not expect the spirits to get along. A relationship can work without divinity, but it will lack the true essence of what you truly need in your lives.

We love to see souls, or, as we call them, spirits, in alignment.

~Ariel~

Angel Blessings

Angel blessings are bestowed upon those who seek them. We seek to shower everyone with the Holy glory of God; this is what we do. We know all of you. We, the Family in the Sky, are asking you to understand this.

~Ariel~

My Life-Mate!

Ray, how many wake up and go to sleep with tears? You are one of them. When we told you someone would be with you for the rest of your life, you became so excited. Now, you are back to tears, and maybe the person we told you about wonders the same way!

I, Ariel, will never tell you anything other than what is for your good. We are life partners, Raymond. When you arrive back in the Sky, I will be there to guide you when you return to Earth for the next trip. I am with you from your first breath to your last. I know you better than you know yourself!

You asked me this morning if your last breath was coming soon. I told you no. We still have work to do together; you, me, and the rest of the family up here. We understand your needs, as well as those of others, and we recognize when they are beneficial or detrimental to you.

Sandalphon and I told you who this person will be. She has the desire, but maybe not the will. We ask you to be willing to adjust to circumstances that hinder your heart. You were chosen to write for us. We chose you to do this. Times are changing quickly, and we desire you to help, along with many others.

Your life mate must be powerful in the arena of love. She will work with you. She will arrive on her white-spirited steed, and her face will shine with the glory of God.

~Ariel, your Angel of eternal forever~

Heartache

As I write this, Ariel tells me that everyone is better off not holding on to anything that is a long-term issue of heartache caused by someone else. You have made great decisions by being alone until your divine moment arrives. Had you not, you may have missed the moment that was meant to be yours.

Choices should not carry fear but hope, for the spirit knows your needs and will search the Earth. You will cross the paths that allow you, and others, to meet on this geometric path of what a righteous heart deserves.

~Ariel~

Ray Kaczar, transcribing Archangel Ariel

March 12, 2025

Ariel's Prophecy: Looking into the Near Future

I, Ariel, an Archangel, will now prophesy a glimpse of what is to come in the not-so-far-away future! History will reveal the entirety of its false teachings, and mankind will begin to desire all that is true.

The Divine entities from the Holy Sky Family will return with light as bright as a thousand suns. Those who thirst for this knowledge shall come to the forefront of its essence. All that was will become all that was always meant to be. This time, however, there will be a stronger desire to live within the Holy plan for life.

-Ariel Arch Angel-

Ray Kaczar; message from Ariel

March 19, 2025

Maybe We Protected You

To move forward, no matter how hard your desire, even if you fail, you have pursued it. Perhaps it did not happen because we protected you.

-Ariel-

Speak Diligently

Good morning. A thought I shared with Ray this morning was this: what comes out of your mouth, the words, will return to your ears from someone else's mouth. Try to speak diligently when speaking to others.

-Ariel-

Your Earliest Families

Visions of Circumstances. Are you drowning in your tears more often than not? Is this self-pity, or are you a victim of the circumstances you accept as life? Humanity is the most precious gift of creation. First came your oceans, and then life began, growing and preparing to sustain a future for human existence. The realms of cosmic desire had arrived.

When mankind was born, they were in the earliest stages of growth and understanding, yet they had the vision to see beyond what they already knew. How could they? The spirits that gave them birth were there to help. Most of you are family to those spirits, and many of you are one of them.

If you knew this, could you ask yourself how much you have evolved as a human? Your existence has often been a mundane experience. Whose fault is this? Is there any true benefit to letting others make your rules for what you are to understand?

From the first breath of any form of life, the Creator God has always given you the gift of free will. So, are you truly living in the freedom of the highest degree, or only what is thought to be freedom?

Transcribing Archangel Ariel

Vengeance

"Vengeance is mine, saith the Lord."

Vengeance is mine, saith the Lord. May I ask all of you—who is your Lord? I already know your answer.

I, Ariel, birthed as an Elohim, know all that you think you realize to be factual. You are spirits, but spiritual desires have remained in stagnation for more than 5,000 years, and still, there is serious digression in what most of you describe as your spiritual connection to the one you choose to worship as God.

Your stories of God's value are worth less than the dollar bills you rely on, just as much as you rely on your God. Concerning the first word, *vengeance*, I will now seek to let understanding become more vivid. In the realm you call Heaven, the Family of Creation would never reverberate a word called vengeance; never.

If you could understand the frequency of the word, you would instantly enter into your higher understanding of all that is. We would welcome you into the world of truth, not what you have been told it is. Clinging to religion to justify wars is an abomination to our pure understanding of everything.

I will tell you that most of you, who have been with us in past lives and desire to return again, are no brighter than your spirit, which shall return again. In plain English: your living spirit, the one who returns as mortal, has the ability to change this return of ignorance.

You have been blessed with a gift that has been pronounced as your key to enlightenment. To find it, you must search deep within your soul. When you do, it will manifest to you more than you may imagine.

I will tell you this: vengeance is your own personal desire, and never will it be a spoken thought from the Most High.

~Ariel~

Programmed! Coded! Manipulated!

Programmed! Coded! Manipulated! This is what the government desires at all levels, from the top to the bottom, an ingenious way to serve themselves.

You are not robots. When they can replace you with machines, what will the next virus become? Humanity, for the most part, has become lazy-minded. Your schools have embedded their agendas, your medical science is manipulated by money, and monstrous corporations control your political leaders.

To put it simply: many have sold their souls to mankind, and for this, you are reaping the crops you have planted. We, the Holy Family, are very disturbed by those who placate and pass on this vermin for life.

You all have been given free will. To rebuild your soul's destiny, you must desire to understand the truth. Most living on Earth are on a downward spiral, which is a reason for living.

The answer is to desire Natural Law, with the understanding that it comes from us, your Holy Family in the Sky.

~Ariel~

Desired Ambition

The ambition of desire, when it is achieved spiritually, will never let you down. It will teach you the truth in the manner that is best for you.

~Ariel~

You Are Responsible for Your Happiness

A principle of my church is this: *you are responsible for your happiness or unhappiness.*

Ariel explained this to me just now: "Okay, Ray, you must learn to abandon what keeps you unhappy. Let it go, and desire to understand this. It has become a common mutation in many people, including you. Strive to be the best version of yourself. Life will become happier. Your decisions are mostly good; be happy, not sad, about them. The glory in your desires can only become reality when, and until, you, or anyone, chooses to follow these natural desires. They are principles and part of what constitutes Natural Law."

~Ariel~

Where Does God Live?

Ray, you ask: *"What if someone asked, where does God live?"*

Here is your answer: God lives in the sky, not just in the universe your Earth is a part of, but in the thousands of universes that exist are home to God. Although this may seem far, you should understand that God also lives within you.

All of you, God gives you a mind that should think unhindered by dogma. Use it!

~Ariel~

Sweet Dreams

Sweet dreams can sometimes be considered a lucid, deep subconscious state, where you see with your eyes closed. Understanding them can be difficult for some, because you may only be willing to see, but not desire to understand.

Some of these dreams can serve as a means of enlightenment, others as warnings, and still others as a way to understand your goals, as well as glimpses of your past and future.

Lucid dreaming is a gift, a tool for humanity.

~Ariel~

Spiritual Bloodlines

Spiritual Bloodlines! Ariel asks me to write her thoughts right now. While all are created through universal or infinite intelligence, many refer to this as God; the understanding is that families were created. In contrast, many understand we are the oneness of the universe in many forms.

This was done through the design of the family. For the sake of unity, the grand design is made up of families that are spirit, which means all of you. Your family spirit has an Akashic bond. This would otherwise be an imperfect design for life.

Your desires for the continuation of humanity are rooted in growth and in understanding the complex energy that you are, just as many families on Earth do. Children multiply, and even then, it is difficult for families to keep track of one another. Many do not even know who their great-great-grandparents were, and some brothers and sisters cannot even keep up with each other's children. Yet these are your family, even if you do not know them.

Just as there are different types of blood, there are also bloodlines of spirit. I am an Angel, and I have the same Creator as all of you. Yes, my being is designed for a different purpose, yet when you transition, you become only spirit again, and you look very similar to me. This makes us into one.

Divineness gives individuals personalities and free thought. Take on the idea that all of you are family and should bless each other with only love, because those of you who claim hatred for another cannot and will not understand how to love themselves.

As Angels were created, so too were some families in spirit, to aid humanity in evolving toward the realization of truth. These bloodlines are essential for maintaining order. Understanding that we are all family is the key to happiness and unity of purpose. Realize your journey in life. Seek the knowledge of truth through us, your Holy Family in the Sky. Ask for the highest and best!

-Ariel-

Justification for the Creation of Humanity

The justification for the creation of humanity is contained in the energies that you cannot see within your planet's atmosphere. I will tell you that one handful of this energy, invisible to your eyes, immediately changes in its way so that it is capable of thinking. It can produce good or bad outcomes because it has free will. This is quantum energy.

It gives the good person as much of a chance at a successful way to understand humanity is now in the process of building what they call quantum computing or artificial intelligence, and that is just what it will become: artificial intelligence dictated by human intelligence. That will always be artificial, or not truthful, intelligence; this becomes limited. Artificial intelligence will always remain something artificial.

It will be the ideal way to control populations from the viewpoint of the government, and it is not limited to some religions. Some of the major concepts of religions contain some of this viper's poison, as their truth is an artificial one.

Has mankind thought it has become smarter concerning its technologies? We understand these goals, but we are not happy about where they are going. The reason for this is primarily that it will affect many humans, indeed, the majority of humanity.

When you live under authoritarian perspectives, you can consider this a doomsday in the making. *But yes, do not be fooled by party colors. They both have the same agendas.* From our perspective, humanity appears in its state with a fragrance of stench; you are being taught to obey only what they want you to learn.

And society as a whole, thanks to the few who did not buy into this programming and understand it, for these people we will admit a higher frequency, because they deserve it.

I recommend that everyone take heed of what the gods of your earth think they can do with your free will. So far, they have been succeeding very successfully in keeping you ignorant of the truth. *See: your future now is heading downhill, while you may see it as going as high as the mountains.*

This technology is being developed solely for profit, and we will allow it to continue. Their strategy has been well planned for thousands of years. As their technology grows, as it has in the past, you must have heard of Atlantis and Lemuria. There are other planets where the same scenario has happened. We let it carry through to see if some beings could wake up, but it was too late. Some did wake up.

The way we see this, your governments and your religions, not all religions, are responsible, but only because the majority lets them become your decision-makers. We are offering a better understanding, but you must deserve it. You must try to earn it by knowing us, by feeling who we are in your heart, and when you are in the totality of this understanding, we will begin to reach out to you.

Is there anything that can make you think of this? It should be your children and their future. Humanity is repeating itself beyond a history that many of you have ever even heard of. It is a highly repetitive, organized method of control. When you agree to live in untruth and do not even question anything except what you're told is the truth, you have purchased that belief.

— *Ariel*

Channeled by Ray Kaczar

June 11, 2025

Transcribed from Ariel Archangel

Relationships?

Relationships are a splendid desire. Some say, *"Let us be married forever."* The spiritual side of love is at an all-time high for many. Many mature and grow into different variations of themselves, and their thoughts and thinking change.

Some walk away from relationships because they see unhappiness growing. This is when happiness turns into sadness. When children are involved, it becomes much more difficult to move on. I have seen many couples stay together for the sake of the children, yet remain unhappy. This, in turn, can make the children sad, as they are aware of their parents' pain.

So, what to do? Decision time arrives. Does one of you stay only for security? Is that trade-off a good decision? Sometimes people choose to stay unhappy, pretending to be happy to others.

Even Angels can feel sadness. So, what is a good resolve? Find your heart, for it contains the ingredients of love. No one should spend most of their life in sadness.

Let me ask you: do you think Father-Mother God will punish you if you grow into a different desire for the balance of your life? If you believe that, then you must feel God is not an understanding God.

The spiritual principles of natural law state that you must be responsible for your happiness or unhappiness. Humans are meant to live in harmony with natural law. Much of our grief stems from the fact that we do not comprehend its power and its love. Partnerships should have mutual desires; otherwise, disaster for the heart can happen.

~Ariel~

Incarnation

There was a time thousands of years ago when an Angel became very close to a human who was not an Angel. They shared a love that seemed to last forever.

This spirit would go back to Earth and take on many vessels of life. The Angel never once took her eyes off this spirit. Even though the Angel incarnated within many humans, as a human, he did not understand this until tonight.

This Angel now declares, *"I love you no matter who you are. When your job is finished one more time, we will spend eternity together as only spirits can. I will protect you until forever."*

~Ariel!

The Vision

The vision of life is as extraordinary as you desire its creation to be. Your destiny is at your command.

Will it always be easy? No. Many lessons are learned because it is not easy. When lessons are realized, destiny changes course for growth.

As you grow, seek happiness. It is up to you to discover what this means. Focus on the natural desires that can create love. The energy of love is the most powerful form of alchemy for change in the universe; it heals everything.

~ *Blessings, Ariel~*

Take on the Day!

Good morning, and blessings from Ariel on this wonderful beginning of a new day.

I just finished telling Ray that many of Earth's issues stem from people's inability to take personal action for change, based on what every mortal should take responsibility for in terms of reform concerning all issues.

I told Ray that you could think of many folks as the walking dead. They let others think for them, and this is not part of natural law.

Blessings! And as Ray would say: *"Now, take on the day!"*

~Ariel~

Careful How You Say it!

Good morning. A thought that came to mind was one I shared with Ray this morning. I told him, *"What comes out of your mouth will return to others' ears from someone else's mouth. Try to speak diligently when speaking to others."*

~Ariel~

2020
Transcribed by Ray Kaczar

Procreation

On Earth as it is in Heaven

Procreation is not only the ability to create, but also to conceive life, and to have the foresight to understand how life must survive and supply the nutrients of life. This has all been given, and everything has procreated. So why are there still issues?

Somebody is listening to the wrong people. What good is it, I ask you, to procreate when the product of procreation cannot see beyond the mirror image of themselves—the one they taught themselves to become?

-Ariel Arch Angel-

"The enclosed warmth, which the earth hath in itself, stirred up by the heat of the sun, assisted nature in the speedier procreation of those varieties, which the earth bringeth forth."

— Walter Raleigh, *History of the World*

Vehemently

Vehemently, based upon passion for understanding truth, is the willingness to delve into the deepest place you have ever dared to go, to understand more than what you have been taught to understand when it comes to understanding life. The code of life is like a code of ethics that all can agree upon: to live harmoniously with one another in equal respect, equal wealth, and equal desire for your neighbors. Anything less than this is straying from the frequencies of divine design. When you craft your thoughts against these frequencies, you short-circuit your understanding.

May 15, 2025

Transcribed by Ray Kaczar, by Archangel Ariel

The Incantation for Life That Is Ready to Invoke Itself for Those Who Desire!

The genius that exists within you, though unrealized by many, has been inhibited by your unwillingness to seek the unknown, and by your acceptance of only what you have been told. That acceptance becomes your reality of truth.

If you feel no more evidence can extend beyond that understanding, then be content with it, for those thoughts have become yours to claim. But what if your knowledge asked you to break the barriers of what seems unchangeable, and to dive deeper to ask: *Am I correct?*

I would begin with the arena of your own thoughts, taking you on a slow journey of growth. Meditate on it. Ask new questions of yourself, including your own Spirit, the one who will carry you to Heaven!

Perhaps your free will itself is holding you back from the truth of all that exists. Your incantation only needs to become a knowledge born of a higher desire for understanding. It is that simple.

Blessings, ~Ariel~

Transcribed by Ray Kaczar, May 27, 2025

Battle Scars of a Child's Life

Battle scars of a child's life cannot simply disappear. The things you have seen should never have become so clear. Your eyes taught your heart deep dismay. You were so young; you could not possibly understand the meaning of child's play. From the start, you were on a trial of trying to run away.

Many could never understand this, especially you. You fought against everything that could have been good with anger and tossed it all away. Your despair nearly brought you to an early death more than once.

You loved the ending of the story of Bonnie and Clyde. When you saw the bullet holes in the movie, you felt them so deeply inside and thought, "*Why can't this be me?*"

Yet you were blessed with a grandmother and an aunt who loved you through it all. From above, they now realize that when they bestowed their love on you, a miracle occurred.

Later, outside a town near Memphis, you were in tremendous pain. You pulled your truck over and cried out to God: *Give me more. I am sorry.* No words were spoken to ask for relief from the pain, but you screamed, "*Please take this life if that is what it takes!*"

We chose this body for you to live in during this journey. We knew the destiny of your growth. It had to be this way, for without it, you could not have become who you are now. Without it, you could never understand what others endure.

You could never feel compassion for the hungry who sleep in the woods and on the streets of the cities. Now, you love to hire those who have made mistakes, and you adore them. Remember the grandmother who thanked you because no one else would give her grandson a chance at work due to his health issues?

As you came to know us more deeply, we fell in love with your requests. We showed and guided you to where you are today. There was a time not long ago, you walked near someone who had a deadly disease. We added a noise in your ear that became louder as you came near him. As you backed up, the noise went away.

You sometimes say to us, *I'm crazy, am I hearing things?* And we reply, "*Why would mediums confirm what you already do and think? This is proof that we are around you every second of every day.*"

Your time could be spent playing and doing what many others do every day, but not you. Instead, you spend it speaking with us almost all day.

Your requests are sincere: to have enough money so that you can build for the cold, the lonely, and the hungry. To form a community and keep sadness far away. You once shouted into the sky: *Give me a small share of what Solomon had, and I will show you what I can do beginning today.*

You even offered us a part of your will. The intent was so strong that we had to test you. You came through. During your tests, people offered to help, but you said, *I will get through this. Your thoughts and caring are more than enough. I am OK.*

Look at what has come from the heartaches of the day. You only ask for one thing, and we understand this as you pray: *She knows who you are, and she will arrive one day.*

~Ariel~

2017

Valuable Integrity

Valuable integrity is the ability to transform the true organics of life energy. Being connected to the frequency of truth is something the world should hunger for, because without it, the world will remain as it is; in constant turmoil.

The process of alignment is not as complicated as one may think. First, there must come the desire to recognize and value truth. This includes using your free will, not to believe everything you have been taught, but to look in the opposite direction and then ask yourself: *Did I make a good choice?* This reflection will bring a whole new perspective, awakening your natural ability to think without the cloudiness of inherited understandings.

The past is like a virus that humanity has accepted. Because of this, you live unconsciously, able only to perform as you are told. Yet so much more exists. Perhaps you will understand this in your next life, yet we would like to see all of you. Try to understand this in the life you have been given, *now*.

Ariel ArchAngel

Transcribed by Ray Kaczar

June 24, 2025

Truth! Where Did It Go?

The quest for accurate truth is becoming a thing of the past. The desire to seek and to understand what truth truly is seems to hold no mental value anymore, as it has become an illusion. Society is losing its sense of true understanding; it is only interested in what you are told to understand.

This may appeal to some, but it only exists as the "truth" they want you to believe. *Who are they? Do we need to elaborate?*

The libraries of the past were destroyed so that those who already understood the truth could ensure you would not. By doing this, they could hoard knowledge and harbor truth from you. Those who think of themselves as "royalty" today continue this diversion, passing on clever deceptions as truth. They write their own version of what they want you to connect to in your understanding.

When was the last sacred text available for you to truly digest?

Upon your Earth, there were once two very sacred places of learning. They were destroyed, and the self-proclaimed monarchies stole the best of their knowledge: the Library of Ashurbanipal at Nineveh (in modern-day Iraq) and the Library of Alexandria in Egypt.

This destruction gave great freedom to write falsehoods; deceptive forces for those of you who have no real desire for truth. You are easily persuaded by those who do not want you to understand. You have inherited their guides and now accept them as your teachers. This new breed of teaching has taken over your minds.

The truth of royalty does not live on Earth as it is portrayed with each new election. It will not take part in the promotion of what they teach you to believe, whether through religion or, in rare cases, spiritual understanding.

Until the heart desires explicit knowledge, and until you ask yourself, *Have I fallen for those who think of themselves as royalty?* you will remain as you are.

-Ariel-

Basic Instinct

Life requires you to incorporate your instincts, then to analyze, to desire, and to acknowledge. If you only live by accepting others' instincts, you have lost the process of your individuality. You have been molded by others.

These rules apply to the very existence of reality.

~Ariel~

Transcribed by Ray Kaczar

June 24, 2025

It Took Me a While, but She Is Now the Best Part of My Life!

Around 2019

Ariel to Ray: I am concerned. All you do is take your every thought and direct it toward us when going to sleep, and when you awake.

Ray to Ariel: Thank you for your concern. I will have it no other way. I am good with having the ability to know my Holy Family at a higher level.

Ariel to Ray: You search for a life mate. Will you slow down when she arrives?

Ray to Ariel: She will be inspired just like me, and we will edify each other to our last breath. We will reach out to God together and serve the Holy of Holies.

Ray to Ariel: Can you find any fault in my desires?

Ariel to Ray: Your love for us is recognized by everyone in the sky who holds the Holy abilities to bring forth the ordained desires of your requests. This is why she is not with you yet; she is rare upon your Earth.

Chapter Eight

The Writings from Seraphim Angel Sandalphon

My Existence

Your existence, Ray, is permanent in our understanding. You must realize that, beyond being mortal, where the perspective of mortality resides in no fear, you are seeking a proper perspective in the human form of breathing: that you need a special human to walk with you.

A mate who will be your lover, mentor, and most spiritual, who desires to know us as you do.

We wish you did not have these desires, for many reasons that are Holy! The one who led you to me is a similar version of yourself in many respects, known as Holy Spiritualism. We understand this need, and the magnetism of the universe has spent much time as a search tool for you. We now understand this need for you as well.

A vision of Holiness is what you represent from deep within your "I AM," and so does she! We are standing aside; you have met her. Now it is time to step up to the plate. As you have done your best, we hope she reciprocates your thoughts. Your souls have already known each other for many centuries; it is no wonder there is sadness.

The Holy Spirit has blessed you with the opportunity to meet again, guiding you to reunite across the entire universe.

~Sandalphon~

The scale of love is weighed by the amount you own, and this is a Natural distribution. Some may have to wait longer for it, but some will grow into their inevitable paths!

~Sandalphon~

Angel Sandalphon, having fun with me about four years ago

March 17, 2025

Ray, you ask me, Sandalphon:

When the Earth begins to resemble Heaven, will we need to eat other life for food?

I tell you, *no*. Your evolution will be like ours in Heaven, with no need for this kind of sustenance.

Your second question: **Whether we are evolving as we should?**

I tell you, *you are not*, because people of the Earth have not yet learned how to break free from mortal rulers and cannot yet see what we desire for you. Again, all of you have free will!

~Sandalphon~

Do you find more happiness while you are sleeping?

Do you realize this? Something rings in my ear, a voice that tells me change is needed; run as fast as you can. Why? Because someday you will fall asleep and not wake up, and in your spirit, you will ask yourself: *So why did you choose what you chose?*

And then, it will be over.

~Sandalphon~

Ray, we could bless you with every gift in the universe. Yet when you wake, you are sad because you do not have the life partner you are searching for. This resonates throughout the Kingdom of Heaven.

We tell you: she is on the way. Your fury for not having her is beyond anything that is considered normal. When she is ready, she will arrive like the winds of a mighty storm. She will not look back, yet this is not fast enough for you!

We understand your needs. Your blessings will enhance like the brilliance of the blue aura you see around all the stars. Stop searching; she already knows you!

~Sandalphon~

What if a mortal takes their own life?

Ray, you asked me today: *What if a mortal takes their own life, versus one who does not?*

The mortal who does not will ascend. Naturally, they have the choice to stay or return to Earth and reincarnate.

Those who end their own life as mortals must return and do it again; there is no choice. You all have jobs to complete!

~Sandalphon~

My Job Is to Bestow Light

Sandalphon is my name. I sit beside God, and I am a Seraphim Angel. My job is to bestow light energy that opens doors to understanding Natural Law to the highest degree.

Yeshua was the last human person who received this gift. As an Essene, he yearned for such understanding from his heart that we enlightened him to a degree no one on Earth has had since. Time has changed since his days, yet many are still tied up in thinking he absolved your sin. Natural Law says you must do this yourself.

He was murdered because he was a threat to the leaders of the part of the Earth he traveled in. So, if you desire such an understanding of the truth, you should mirror his desires, along with those of his wife, Mary, and the rest of his most holy group with whom he lived and traveled.

What good is this information? You should figure this out on your own. When you do, you will understand that you should not choose unnatural versions of the Holy Natural Law that was meant to be your guide for life.

For glory to exist in men, the man must yearn for it. And until then, we are going to work with very select Mortals to help this Earth yet once again. Time has arrived!

~Sandalphon~

Humanity Must Strive for the Common Good!

I will declare, Ray, that there are millions of star systems, as well as universes, that contain life. Earth is far from the only one.

Now think about the jobs we have in your Sky Family! We love all of these as much as we love Earth. Many of these planets have inhabitants who have evolved to such a high level that they reside in higher dimensions. Earthlings should be doing the same, yet many seem not to desire the understanding that they have a responsibility to seek this knowledge.

~Sandalphon~

The Test!

When any Spirit comes through to ask Ray to Angel Write or Ascended Master, no matter who it is, they have something to say that carries only positive notes.

He has uncomfortable feelings concerning Lucifer asking him to write a few words, but we asked him to write them!

Ray was tested by us when he offered some compelling words last January. We took them very seriously. He lost his property, including his building, tools, and office, with no insurance to help him through. He stood in the snow, looked at the wood burning in flames, and said:

"I know why you did this to me. I will not rescind my words to you. You can kill me right now, but my words will not be changed!"

I will say to all of you: We, including Mother-Father God, were gathered together, watching this ordeal of flames consuming what seemed like everything to him, to see what would come from his mouth, conceived in his heart. Most of us bet against him, including me.

That night in bed, he summoned Lucifer to face him, and Lucifer did just that. He came to him in spirit. Ray said these words to him:

"You did this to me, didn't you?"

Lucifer said: *"Yes, I did! For your mouth and heart uttered some of the most powerful words to us. I, the Tester of those who will reveal your truth, have caused this to happen to your business. You will rebuild, and your most Holy Sky Family will now realize they can trust your desires."*

To seek the highest, you must realize your heart must be part of the desire. It will be tested for why you want what you desire. Any of you who wish to understand your reason for being on Earth, it begins with striving to make Earth as it is in Heaven.

I am Sandalphon. I sit next to God, and this gives me the responsibility of understanding and serving the highest.

Ray again feels that I should not share my thoughts on this Angelic message. I am doing this because I want all of you to see that you do not need to read all the mythological stories of the past. You are seeing this Holy story of the journey of birth in the now.

The linear year is called 2021 on Earth!

~Sandalphon~

Looking into an Akashic Soul's Past

It can only be considered a blessing when we reveal your history, your reasoning for understanding this, and your desire. They merge with your truth, and you will be shown this knowledge so that it magnifies the advancement of your present.

Father-Mother God, let this happen as a gift for us to reveal. These are stored memories that can help us interpret our mortal future.

For some, it may be necessary to show pieces at a time, because the ability to digest information can lead to misunderstanding or misinterpretation.

As well, why would you desire to know where your spirit has been in the past? For fun, or for creating a better future to help make Earth evolve as it is supposed to? We would call this growth.

~Sandalphon~

A Soulmate

It is a partnership that is not new in any form; it evolved alongside you. Now and then, people in your current life can reap the results of former times.

Your soul or spirit mate has a destiny to collide with you, depending on the journeys you take in every reincarnation. It can be a tremendous opportunity to embark on a blissful partnership in life for mortals.

What if you are in a life partnership, and now your soulmate has already manifested? Does this meeting of the souls unite, and do you walk from the past?

I would say it should be your choice, but think diligently. Your soul and your soulmate have been searching for each other for a long time. If you are content and in love, stay where you are.

Did your soulmate understand you were not, and did your spirit show your soulmate how to find you?

Creator God has given all of you soulmates. Relationships were meant to be loving and fulfilled. Does this make it a Holy relationship? All relationships should be Holy, because that is how you all are designed!

The holiness of the air is life. The breath of air you inhale should bring happiness, because it is the Holy gift of life.

A soulmate is an ignition of togetherness beyond anything, because it is by design. Yet you have a choice: desire to seek and fulfill, or stay as you are.

~Sandalphon~

Galactic Fight!

Angel Sandalphon asks me for a fight

Galactic Fight?

Ray, if you and I were to go at it, who would come out on top?

Sand! Are you saying *InSpirit against InSpirit?* I would say maybe you, but that is a maybe.

Ray, I would. Yet when we were done, I admit I would be tired. You know, Ray, we have fun together, and this could never really happen because this isn't what we do up here. Yet I love watching you watch the Ali fights. I asked you because I know how strong your Spirit is.

When your fire took your Spirit to tears, you shouted back with strength and honor to us!

So, Sand, I'll ask Ariel for her opinion, if you don't mind. Ariel, who would win?

I would, Ray, because I wouldn't let either of you fight. I love you both way too much!

~Sandalphon and Ray and Ariel~

Temporary Journey

Life as a human is a temporary journey; it is meant for the soul to be happy. If you are not content, then it becomes your essence. You can change it.

Time is not on anyone's side if you spend it feeling sad! We are aware of all the reasons humans become sad. Most of them are because of guilt in a current situation: fear to act, fear that maybe there is a reason you feel miserable, and the inability to gain courage because guilt holds you back.

Guilt is energy that tells you *better not move forward.* It loves for you to remain in the place you don't want to be, it owns you!

Run from these chains, and you have a good chance of being very happy!

~Sandalphon~

Love Is Such a Precious Gift

The return of love is such a precious gift. All the value it displays can change the world. When two people offer love to each other, they can change their lives from sadness to joy.

When two people love Holiness, they can live with lasting, divine, lifelong sharing of contentment. I say to you: contentment matched with love adds up to the reason you were born.

This kind of match-for-life partnership only comes along rarely! Chase it down if you are searching.

~Sandalphon~

Ray Kaczar

Transcribing the Angel Sandalphon

Holy Natural Law

Understanding Begins with Nature

Holy Natural Law 1

The universal language of Natural Law is vast. Yet it works in all systems of life, within all planetary existence, in any universe and beyond.

Understanding that the creation of everything in existence is divine, by the very nature of the way it has been created, the desire for this understanding is the first step in reaching out. The benefit of this brings joy and penetrates the dark teachings of anything less than light!

Holy Natural Law 2

The understanding of Law Number 1 allows you to realize the need for the existence of a rule that overrides unnatural or man-made laws that reflect untruth or selfish, ego-based rules.

Holy teachings are Holy Law. We guide you to divine understanding so that your habitat may become as it is in Heaven. For this to manifest, one must first show the ability to begin to understand Law Number 1. And to understand anything, you must yearn to know us, the creators of the law, your life, and the place where you live this life!

Natural Law 3

Healing in the entirety of consuming Angelic energy is a gift from us. All humans have healing energy. The more you strive to understand your divine ability, the more powerful your ability becomes!

The degree of this blessed gift depends on who you realize you are, and who you desire to become. Your healing energy is powered through the vibrations of Holy energy. We gave you natural healing ability at birth. Alchemy is the essence of who you are.

At times, it may need a tune-up, and healers can modify the alchemy for others.

Angelic Healing is an energy we are involved with. Yeshua, for instance, was a healer gifted with this Angelic, supercharged ability. He lived to understand Natural Law, while the law of mankind lived in fear of his powerful understanding of it.

My question to all is this: why did the law of mankind fear the healing abilities of Yeshua and his desire to understand Natural Law?

Sandalphon

Chapter Nine

Socrates

Holy Cosmic Reset
I Chose Poison

In the midst of what I deem the creation of new thinking, advantageous events begin with a deep withdrawal from centuries of schooling that have failed humanity. This is nothing new; nearly 3,000 years ago, this same teaching existed and remains to this day. I was willing to digest poison rather than beg for mercy from a court with a political mindset that had doomed me from its inception.

Every court of law or political group must present an excuse to permit itself from treason. Global institutions have learned this from us and from others of our time. Wealth and privilege were the doctrines of having gained executive privilege. In our time, if you did not worship the gods they told you, you were deemed a heretic.

Let me ask you before we continue: have you fallen into this category, more than 3,000 years later? So, let me ask again, have you fallen into the snares of what you are told to understand, which is anything but what they tell and sell you?

~Socrates~

Ray Kaczar Transcribing Socrates

Precious Thoughts

As a person who used to teach my most precious thoughts, all of these years later, nothing much has changed. The biggest changes I have found lie in the fact that they have polished their lies and deceptive forces through glamour and glitter. Hoping for change without money is almost useless.

Despair is spreading rapidly across humanity. This saddens me at a time when humanity has progressed so well, with many wonderful inventions. The one thing that will never change is the assumption that some of the most vicious human beings on the Earth seem to be able to process and establish control over humanity; clever, ingenious, and with the wealth to do as they please, while you are lucky to buy groceries without getting a loan.

The corporate viciousness is disgusting to my eyes. Yet we are in the Earth's favor of justice, and we are diligently seeking repercussions for the selfish changes that are coming soon. This will alleviate much sadness. The changes will incorporate the spiritual essence, which has never been truly understood by most people.

I ask those who have never understood this to become open-minded. It is imperative

Your Smile Tonight

Your smile tonight lights up the heavens. We wish you joy this evening, Ray. You are happy for a change, and I ask why. Vibrations have reached us, but don't say we don't keep an eye on you all the time!

Ray, you say you know who I am, but ask me not to tell you until it is time to sign my name. You said I am not Hermes, and I tell you that you are correct. You say you feel philosophy in me, and I said you do? Then you say, "*Do you know philosophy?* I say, *yes, a little bit!* And you say, "*Would you shed some of your brilliance in this writing?* So, I say, *yes, I will try!*

An ability to decipher words from the Holy Kingdom is so valuable in that its riches are not of gold nor silver but in love! I ask your readers: does a trip to and winning everything in Las Vegas hold more wealth than receiving a single blessed message from the Kingdom of all that is Holy?

Treasure that manifests in the chakra called the heart is the wealthiest place on earth; you do not even need luck to win. You all have been given a heart, yet you do not understand its most actual treasure: the vibrations of love.

Since one person at a time may begin to realize this, it has all the potential on earth to become such a place that you will never need Las Vegas to find happiness.

Ray, you call me "Grumpy" sometimes! I know I was unpleasant at one of the times we channeled, and I must say that when I was mortal, I was indeed Grumpy at times. You make me happy when you remind me of myself: goodnight, my friend.

~Socrates~

Ray Kaczar

April 2, 2025

Socrates came in at 4:38 a.m.

Thank you, Ray, for having me in your group this morning. I must admit that you have certainly advanced since the first time you worked with Susan and I. We did such a long session in channeling. I am thinking all the questions you asked me, and I realized that you never desired anything for yourself;, was always about how we up here could make things better for humanity.

I started to show you some truth in mythological teachings, that your world has so much of. I know you are tired right now, and as we tried not to get involved with your sleeping habits this morning, you insisted that if anyone wanted to say something, let it be said! I took the opportunity to offer a few words.

My final words for the day are these: you have done more than any of us ever asked of you in your Sky Collective. Though I may have been grumpy with you, I want you to know I love you. I, with thousands of other Sky family members, am watching your every breath you take.

I want to say this is why your Lady is not with you yet; she is on Earth right now. This means you are not meant to be with just anyone. We have chosen someone for you. We consider her a Queen of the Sky family, and when she lets you know who she is, you will thank us for the long wait. Please, Ray, do not stop being you!

Ray, I considered myself a wise man as a human, and I could not laugh at stupidity. However, when I watched you play that YouTube video with the Three Stooges with Moe getting his head stuck in a pipe, you had me laughing for a long time. It helped me get off my high horse as well.

Blessings to all who are in this group. Knowledge from the Sky is falling upon everyone who seeks it. We adore all of you!

~Socrates~

Ray Kaczar

Transcribing Socrates this morning through automatic writing
March 18, 2025

Vehement

My learning of Stoicism remains a vehement passion.

The vehemence that exists within my mind, and of my mind, is a desire for the ability to describe what is key, for understanding. This is still who I am.

Don't settle for what everyone tells you to believe. If you are unwilling to question, you may not be living your own life; it may be one that society has chosen for you!

Yet, when desire becomes void in your understanding, you must accept the result of continuation: that everything will stay as it is.

Ray Kaczar

April 2, 2025

Border Land

Channeled to me by Socrates

Nations that will not respect the borders of others will ultimately lose. Disrespecting and forcing one's own will, from one government to another, is a disgrace to any nation that desires honor!

~Socrates~

Chapter Ten

Marcus Aurelius
Seek Dignity, Not Gold!

Transcribing Marcus Aurelius

Marcus Aurelius has a few words he would like to share:

"When a man possesses dignity, his true value is worth more than any amount of gold. He does not seek for his fellow citizens to become his servants or to call him master. What he would only want for himself is the ability to give others a better life, a deeper understanding of life, and a commitment from the heart that is filled with virtue. Anything less than this does not qualify anyone to run any country at any time in history, or in the future.

I did not fit into this category. That is because I did not know this when I returned to this earth. I will bring my knowledge with me. I wish all of you could develop a desire for such knowledge. You have every right to listen to what you are told or to evaluate what you are told from a governmental perspective. If you are happy with what is happening, live with it, but make sure it is acceptable for your children's future, and theirs.

There is no one up here who is very impressed with the choices many of you make. There is nothing wrong with making mistakes or bad choices, but when you cannot change your way of thinking to make this earth a more loving place, you have not truly committed; you have let others make your decisions for you!

When your mind becomes part of another person's mind that contains values less than virtue, and you adopt their way of thinking, it does not say much for you!

These are my thoughts; think what you may. I would rather make people angry and wake up, and have people who are alive more ignorant than the spirits you call dead!

—Marcus

Transcribing Marcus Aurelius,

June 26, 2025, by Ray Kaczar

A Very Personal Chat with Marcus

Marcus: Hello, Raymond. You know very little about my history. Your concerns about your understanding of me are accurate. I was never a self-proclaimed perfect leader. I had my own personal issues, my own demons within me, and plenty of demons around me all the time. These could be considered political demons; they called themselves advisors. Ask me some questions, please!

Raymond: Marcus, I would like to ask you questions about what we are facing in our modern history. It really is not much different from your time, just the weapons we use are so much more advanced and dangerous. My first question is this: You have so much experience watching history from high above. You can compare this concerning warfare, because you were involved in so much warfare in the past. What can you tell me about what is going on today?

Marcus: You have asked me this question so eloquently. I feel you did not put me on the spot, but I am not afraid to be put on the spot for the things I did not do correctly. I admire you for this. Your distinct love for the Earth surpasses anything that I possess by far. I did not understand who the true God or Creator was, and still, as it always will be, you see through this with open eyes and a beautiful heart.

I carry guilt to this day for the things I have done wrong, but I also carry sorrow in my heart. As we speak together, I am watching very closely what is going on throughout the Earth because, in some ways, I feel responsible for many who copied my strategies.

I don't think I am a bad or cruel person, but I made many mistakes and bad choices along with the good ones I made for my people. During my time, I was surrounded by political deception and monsters. Your president is not only surrounded by them. He is one of them. Every one of them in your modern leaders has been a greedy and selfish human being!

We did not possess a corporate structure as strong and designed to control as there is in your lifetime. The only thing that may be different or more modern is your ability to dominate others through the monetary system, and in a much more advanced way. Looking in both directions, the past and the future, I see a very great need for people to understand and seek the highest truth, to ask and beg for it to be shown and distributed, and then to teach it to the children, so this cycle can finally come to a halt.

I spend a lot of time as a spirit now, but I am very active because I have a love for the truth, just as you do. The suspense of keeping people divided is as powerful as a nuclear weapon; it keeps the citizens of every government in line. Humanity is basically a servant to the elite, and what is interesting to me is the fact that the majority of human minds are clouded in the name of religion. Religions are meant to teach obedience in diverse ways, yet people cannot see the reasoning behind this art of control. It allows the elite to maintain their structure of power. It actually takes great pleasure in watching their strategy continue and prevail, keeping the population, including many educated people, numbed in their thinking.

Dialect, if it goes in the wrong direction against what people believe they have been taught, causes conflict. The majority of humanity in every country or nation sets a snare in their own minds, so they essentially cave in to what their government tells them to understand. Every government is intelligent enough to know how to control its own citizens: they make you desire more, purchase more. The art of money is always in their favor. *Spend, and we will lend you the money to buy what you need.*

Your natural instincts become influenced by their processes. Watching you, I can tell you understand this now. You are battling this process yourself. You have tried to play their game. I will openly state that I know for a fact our Creator has taken this from you so that you may learn what truly is supposed to be.

You have had a hard time adjusting, yet you have tried with an open heart and a willingness to do so. I'm not sure I would have had that willingness during my life on Earth.

The talk up here is constant: massive groups from the angelic side and those who once lived on Earth, who are constantly thinking about how the earth can become as it was supposed to be. We are not allowed to force this. In the organization called Divinity, we have strict ethics that we must live by

You are struggling with this in your own personal spirit, but you knew and understood this already. There is a Galactic Federation, a group of many nations that reside on thousands of other planets within and beyond your solar system. They are advanced, and they do not like cruelty; they do not approve of what is happening on Earth. Some of their leaders, generals of galactic functions, have come to you and told you to maintain your way of thinking.

You have been very sick, yet you are doing the best anyone could ever ask of you. From our group high above, you are being accused of spending too much time with us. You are starting to feel a touch of guilt. I am asking you to stand strong. Your stoic abilities are growing. Your fears, which are very valid concerning your personal life, are well known to everyone up here who watches you and works with you diligently.

Your health will return to the point where you can be content once more. I will end this with words I must tell you: you are much loved. I only wish I could have had love for humanity as you do.

In closing, Raymond, let me tell you something: in all my time since ascension, I have watched every leader, warmonger, and greedy financial distribution system diligently. Let me tell you, I am proud that you represent us as an Earthling.

Transcribing Marcus Aurelius,

By Ray Kaczar, June 18, 2025

Chapter Eleven

Metatron
Ray Kaczar

Automatic writing from Metatron

March 18, 2025

Veil of Darkness

Archangel Metatron will be speaking to me now. He tells me he has concerns and would like to share them.

Ray, this is a special day for you. You thought you were only going to clean and work, yet since your visit to a church, you have not stopped for as much as a minute, being fully involved in your desire to know and share in our mutual love.

You asked Ariel if anyone would care to share the thoughts or concerns we may have up here. I raised my hand the fastest, as many yearn to share truth within our Holy Community in the sky, so to speak.

I would like to highlight the need to understand the Holy essence of our family, or what you call the *Sky Family*. Our desires are most definitely intended for those who truly seek the knowledge of what it will take to mend all the untruths that have brought hardship upon the Earth.

This was never meant to be. In the beginning, there was no desire for life to ever know sickness, hardship, or despair. Mankind was given the choice to live as they desired. Many thought they should become better than others and deserved more as well. There was also interference, this darkness being invaded by other life forms from other star systems.

All of you are genetically modified hybrids. This means your lineage began with life from these other systems. Some were controllers; some were not. This is what happened. We watched this with intensity. Humanity had a brain capable of understanding this, yet not all chose to do so. Some thought the rest should serve them.

The law of Nature has been on Earth since day one. Some understood they were Star seeds. They were clever. So let us move forward to where all of you have evolved. Because you still have your free will, humanity has gone backward, and many do not realize this!

We are extremely saddened that the children whom God created still act not much differently than they did at the very dawn of creation. If, for one second, you think otherwise, you will fit right into the dark hands of the evil that lurks. This evil understands, and it has the ability to abuse a good soul, because they prey on this, feed on this, and devour this. Your entity is a slave to them.

Atlantis had knowledge beyond your current capabilities, and they also thought they should believe in themselves. It was so sad that they had to fall. Our Mother-Father Creator is deeply sorrowful that this continues. Yes, they can change this instantly, but then your free will would disappear. That would make you like Droids. This will not happen. So, all of you must desire understanding beyond that of mankind. Our message for humanity is this: until you seek and ask for understanding of the truth, you will remain floating in a swamp of deception and live the way you so desire.

It is your will to make a change. Become a free thinker, that would be my suggestion. Use what you were blessed with. This is a serious situation. Ask and pray to be shown understanding, and if you seek it, it will arrive faster than you can even speak the words!

Your divinity requires understanding. All it takes is to ask these words:

Holy Father, Holy Mother who art in Heaven, thy Kingdom will come. Please, we beg you, break the veil of darkness so that we may shine in the building of Your Kingdom on our Earth.

~Metatron~

Metatron

As a human, my name was Enoch. My desire for understanding God and the Holy Community was so strong that they took me under their wings. I had to transition, as humans do, into the fullness of Spirit. In my case, our Mother-Father was very proud of my quest or thirst to understand the truth of all that is.

They gifted me with an angelic essence and crowned me with the title of Archangel, giving me the name Metatron. I do my best to serve and love the fact that many can understand my desire to assist in everything that must continue for the reality of all that is, and all that must arrive to fulfill the words: *"Thy Kingdom come, on Earth as it is in Heaven."*

All of you are responsible for making this task arrive!

-Metatron-

Transcribed by Ray Kaczar, about 2020

Channeling Metatron

Chapter Twelve

John the Baptist

Baptism

John speaks of Yeshua's Baptizing

My name is John, and I would like to speak for a few moments about life in the days when I walked the earth. I was what you call a spiritualist today. I lived each moment, giving my all to the Holy Spirit, Mother, and Father God. As I grew into a young man, an Angel approached me to baptize in the name of the Holy Spirit. I was a loner as a child. I knew my life would be spent teaching others how to walk in the Spirit.

Baptism is an enlightenment for the hope that one can reach out in life and realize the calling of the Holy Spirit to enhance every desire they created for all of us. Mythological writings have told an untrue version of my life on earth, but I have indeed baptized Yeshua. I will tell you that you can baptize yourself by wanting to become a human who desires to understand this Holy United Kingdom of God, how? Just expect it, and thy will shall be done!

~ John the Baptist ~

Ray Kaczar

Auto-writing with John the Baptist

About 2022

John the Baptist

Mythology

I asked Ariel if anyone with you cares to do some auto-writing. I had to ask her four times if I had the name correct. "Ok, Ray, let go. Your abilities to do this writing, I have had my eyes on you for some time. I see that you care for the enlightenment of the earth folks to understand why the earth is in such disarray. The time has changed so much since the days I have walked the earth plane, yet in many ways, it has not changed at all, in my time they were busy building their environment of control and deceit, now they are getting lost in what the truth can ever be, the truth to many has become the best way to deceive, and make it sound honest!

Ray, the way you believed in Ariel, many think that my story is as real as everything you thought to be true. Mythology is hard to disprove when it becomes thousands of years old. Myths say that I was beheaded in prison, but this never happened; I died from old age, a natural transition. Life was hard in those days as well. My whole life was to serve the Father-Mother God, and I have done just that. You knew me in those days, though it is not yet revealed to you. I admire your desire to share the truth to shine; it is the only way to make the earth a place that it is supposed to be. This is our first chat; I look forward to doing this much more as you progress in understanding and knowing us. In truth, we are all very old friends of yours, Ray."

Blessings to all!

~John the Baptist~

Chapter Thirteen

Jophiel, Archangel

Abraham Sending His Child to Death

Ray, you sent a deer to his death in a dream this morning. You woke up asking what this meant. This deer followed you into a building, and a human wearing white was following you. When you entered inside, the other human cut the deer, and you blamed yourself. You demanded an explanation.

You felt it was your fault; he died for no reason. You asked the Creator to help you. God told you to learn a lesson concerning sacrifice: get a clear definition.

Now take this deep into your I Am and tell me what comes to your mind. You said, "Abraham." You asked God, "Did you tell him to sacrifice his son?" And God said, "Yes, I did." And you said, "I do not understand why you would do this!"

Later, when God let you dwell upon this, He revealed it was a test for Abraham. He asked you what you would have done. Your words were: "Why would he kill his son, when he should have said, 'I will do better and take my own life.'" You thought of him as a coward.

You see, Ray, that is why I had to put the lamb in front of him.
~ Jophiel, your teacher of wisdom and truth ~

A gift you call the Stone Angel:

You told her you had been staring at her most of the day. She, who gifted you this, told you to ask what she wants. Ray, you did this, and I came to you. You asked, "Who are you?" I told you to go to your deck of angel cards and pick one; these are another gift. You chose me, Jophiel, an angel who teaches wisdom and the beauty of God.

We have been together endlessly through the centuries; you did not know this, as you do not retain the past unless we show it to you.

Is it not amazing that a gift of a card and an angel of stone was used to inspire me to reach out to you? Knowing us is not a matter of magic or luck. There are things we will not do, and one of them is that we will not infringe on anyone's life unless they invite us in.

Guardian angels are with you. Consider asking them to reveal themselves to you, telling them you desire to get to know them, and inviting them into your heart; they have much to offer.

The more you desire to understand the other side, the more time you dwell in the airspace owned by heaven, and you can achieve much greater happiness. So, I ask: what is wrong with that?

~ Jophiel ~

Holiness versus Spiritualness

For this evening, your thoughts on holiness versus spiritualness, and combining them into a love affair with God's essence, are powerful.

Ray, you say to me, "Why do people go to church and pray for forgiveness each week and then carry on just as they did the week before?" I say this, in many instances, because they fear a place called Hell. Some seek to love, although they might not give love equal to what they desire. Part of the heart wants to love, and part wants to forget that understanding is more than they understand, because the heart is only partially in a desire to know God and family.

~ Jophiel ~

A Rare Gift

One must realize that the other side can and will bring love to those who dwell in loving us in the sky. When you know us, we let you understand that you are fulfilling all that you should be in your part of the scheme of making, or syncing, the geometry of such love affairs.

Now, I, Jophiel, say that if you will not grab this rare gift, then its energy will dissipate and move to new circuits. These feelings or energies are gifts; they are spiritual gifts for those who earn them.

~ Jophiel ~

Is your truth deceptive?

Beyond all that is thought of as the reasoning of the justice of truth, that can respond with the resonance of mythological story, is beyond the ability to ask, "What am I being told? Is it deceptive?"

~Jophiel~

Natural Law

Understanding nature's processes is growth. You start to escape the process of mankind's teachings about life versus the understanding of the spiritual side of life, your everlasting version.

~Jophiel~

In times of loneliness, the horizon can share the most beautiful dreams that may become a reality for life-lasting requirements.

Trusting in God is the first step in the search for what one may need. God understands your desires, as well as proportion the deserved amount to the understanding that you may understand!

Dividends concerning relationships are as powerful as the market for understanding the value that you are willing to be happy with.

Blessed are those who can rise and understand!

~Jophiel~

Chapter Fourteen

Writings from Michael ArchAngel

Early this morning, I asked you to write each word. As you read this, you will see a glimpse of our history and all we have accomplished together as a collective. This is a broadcast of teamwork by a human working with his Holy family in the sky. We desire that the humanity of the earth operate in this manner.

You have a rare desire to serve our Creator-Father. Unlike many, you witnessed a table lifting in the air the first time you channeled. It meant nothing to you; your desire was only to understand the highest and best, and still is! This showed us who you have become. Your only purpose in being at the session was to get to know us.

~Michael~
About 2020

Ray, as we have our conference this evening, I want to say that we watch the intent of your every breath and thought with the precision of analyzing your every move. When I first appeared to you as a human, you looked me in the eye, and I stared with a gleam at you, thinking it has been such a long time coming for this day to happen, your request for Father God to be in complete charge of your desires was a request we have desired for so long, your intent is for zero selfishness,

Then came last New Year's Day, and what you gave me was something I have never had anyone offer me for the proper reasons that you did. We have taught you how to understand us now; our communications are almost like two humans using a cell phone, and this only improves as we move forward. You have had a large request from Our Father. Your sincerity was so real, and it has not flickered, even though you battled the fiery tests of your life in the last year. I bet on you, Ray

Every day, you go through lessons that we teach you, you must learn now so that as your desires expand, you will be strong like me and face the choices I must make as an Angel as well. Ray, I asked you to write this down for many reasons, and I must tell you the same thing that Mother-Father and Ariel have told you: your personal desire for a life partner is rare on this earth today. Mother told you we had chosen such a lady for you; she will be to you as you call an earth angel, and Ariel told you the lineage of Mary Magdalene was walking this earth yet today, so for now, you are in our schoolroom, and your report card is an A-plus!

~Michael~,

I have been in conversation with Michael since 12:10 a.m. last night. I fell asleep while with him for an hour or so; this is the last question I asked him this morning. "Michael, you and the rest of the angels, all the Ascended Masters, etc., in Heaven, do you still worship Father-Mother God, and are you that close to Him?"

Ray, we reside with Him. God gives us no dogma, and we are to distribute His love. It has all the power and the glory that can never be matched by anything. Love and its resonance in everything! You and humanity, including us, are his prodigy! Whosoever desires His I

Am shall find it, for the light He shines is available to all life. Yes, we worship Father-Mother God!

~*Michael*~

Chapter Fifteen

Miscellaneous Messages from Angels, Ascended Masters, and Others

Mysteries and Myths: Who Is Yaldabaoth?

The God you choose to believe in, those you may think of as divinity in its highest form, virtue in its purest sense, most of us believe in something. I am not one of them anymore.

Consider the God of the Bible. Leave the god Jesus out of it and go back to one more ancient figure: the god who today is claimed by both Islam and Christianity, Yahweh. This being, I argue, was of human origin.

Before Yahweh could win the title of the God of Judaism, he had to challenge another already chosen deity: a god called El. This early group, seeking a single god, became known as monotheistic. In the end, they chose Yahweh. Yahweh was considered the god of war, and still is.

Yahweh is one of the more modern gods in human history. He has only been worshipped as a singular God for about six hundred years beyond the time of the god later Christianized as Jesus. The governments of those times, the monopolies of strength, chose who their gods would be.

Take Socrates, for example. He was executed for telling people they did not have to believe in the gods of Athens. History claims there have been thousands of gods. I once asked Siri how many; I think she said thirty-three million throughout time.

The God of the Bible seems the most popular in modern times, but according to some Gnostic traditions, his image has been shaped by the archons. These beings, who think of themselves as gods, are what Edgar Cayce called "material-world demons." They hold us hostage. We always owe somebody something. As long as we're alive, we are in debt to the gods of money and so forth.

These archons are teachers of deception to the highest degree. Through deception, they keep you exactly where they want you. No matter how intelligent or educated you are, you can be caught in their realm of ignorance.

In modern times, consider the monopoly of corporate structures. Let me ask you to think carefully before you answer: do you believe these board members, the stockbrokers, these deceivers, and the manipulators of man-made money might be under the influence of the archons?

I admit I am not well-versed in the full history of these gods; the seven gods of seven planets. But the one who created them, if I have the stories right (and I believe I do), was named Yaldabaoth. He made the others and considers himself the true God: the mastermind of deception.

They have agreed to channel through me; Yaldabaoth will speak on behalf of all of them.

So, here we go.

You are heavenly, and your earthly desires are very interesting. I had to gather with my comrades and see what you could tell us about us. We are known as the deceivers. I can assure you that we do not deceive. We tell our story, and your humanity buys it. We take great pleasure in seeing how ignorant humanity has become throughout the ages. Most of you have peaked; you are also easy to control.

The ones you think of as the elite or the government of the world are equally as stupid. They are willing to do anything for the cornucopia of treating others in such a bad way with such cleverness that we teach them that they are equally as ignorant as the ones they portray to become as they desire for their glory, for their wealth, their desire desires their words speak untruth, but humanity's stupidity is not smart. Those who are not educated enough to see through this are not to blame, so this does not make it our fault.

From our perspective, we take great pleasure in the invocation that is so easily pronounced within your little tiny minds. With all due respect to you, we will tell you that humanity is our entertainment, so let me ask you, does this make us that terrible just because the majority of you are so gullible? We forced nothing on no one. Humanity has openheartedly received our frequency upon your earth. I have nothing to lie to you about. I think this is surprising to you, and I think you will have some respect for my truth. This is why I chose to speak with you tonight. I'll be on behalf of my family, on behalf of my nature, and on behalf of my view and perspective.

I must say to you, thank you for your invitation to speak with us. I understand you have asked another spirit if we would gather and speak to you. We have done that now, and we appreciate the opportunity. Dignity is rarer than gold upon your earth, yet you prefer gold over dignity or virtue. When I speak of gold, I mean anything that can be purchased with gold for your pleasure. Your desire for pleasure comes at such a price that many of you cannot ever afford it, so you buy it and you pay our comrades who live on the Earth sometimes more than twice as much, and you wonder why you are living in such a way that you do.

I speak proudly at this moment. I am not ashamed, as you have asked me when we first began our conversation this evening. I will consent that we may become known as instigators. Yeah, nobody is twisting anyone's arm and forcing anyone against their free will; they chose to live in the zone of life. Their choice can change, yet we do not see this happening. You're thinking right now. Why would the creator allow this? I will tell you that your free will, as you know and understand to a very high degree, is of great importance to the Creator Source.

We exist for the reason that exposes the stupidity, the ignorance of centuries of humanity's growth. Please let me terminate our conversation. I am very honored that you approached me and my comrades. I will be happy to speak to you in the future. If need be, I will tell you bluntly, as you asked me if I carried any shame; my answer is no. Humanity has become so manipulated by us from our perspective. We see it as your fault if you want to purchase this deception; we will sell it to you. We have been backlogged for a long time. We have no surprises.

I do understand you're going to become a roadblock in our way. I can tell you that I have respect for you; your frequencies, which give you life, are special. I can tell you hail to anyone who has a desire to break away from false truth! We understand it; we do not even live by our deceptive practices. On behalf of my truth, which is something rare for the Earth ever to be administered. I must tell you, humanity deserves everything it deserves. Your minds are lazy. They are disgusting to my eyes.

You think you are creators and, in some respect, you purchase almost anything that your religion or your government wants to sell you. Our human counterparts equally enjoy deceiving and reaping the rewards of your hard work. We have nothing to hide from you. You can ask me any question you like, and I will stand up to you and give you the best answer that I know how. I will speak to you as others do, so that you can understand in your own words. I must tell you that I am more than amused by our conversation. I was not sure how you would respond. You are asking me if there are any antidotes to what I'm telling you, and in simple Terms, I must tell you that you must desire truth to the highest degree, yet you already understand this.

I will leave you alone at this point, and I thank you for this opportunity. I also know you're thanking me right now for my honesty with you.

Artor, my newfound Pleiadian friend

Last evening, Raymond, we had a brief but very pleasant conversation. Your understanding and your courage to speak on behalf of so many throughout the solar system are heartening. It gives us hope to see a human voice reaching for truth, one step at a time, one star at a time.

Why do people fear? Why are they afraid to commit to this search, to ask themselves, *Is there a better way? Have I been lied to? Am I being controlled? Am I living in a prison without bars?*

We understand how this came to be through the ages. Your system is horrendous; humanity has been steeped in darkness since ancient times. Over the centuries, control has tightened, shaped by religion, enforced by governments. Your religions fear speaking its full truth, lest the state strip away its privileges. Your judicial systems are wildly out of balance. Your monetary system, soaked in manipulation, is painful for any human to face, let alone to live within.

Last evening, as you gazed at the stars, I appeared to you for a moment. Not in full form, but you saw me standing on the ground. You rose from your chair and came toward me with a hug. That was a first for me.

You asked about the vessels you had seen the night before, moving quickly through the starlight. You wondered if they were Reptilian craft. My answer is yes. In a few days, they will arrive. They are battle-ready. A deep darkness travels with them.

This is a polite way to describe how the indignities of life reach your Earth. Yet let me explain: they are not specifically concerned with your planet. They aim to dominate all matter. Many humans are born into a system that carries the genetics of these dark, individual souls.

What you consider a *galactic community* is very real, and at this moment, it is deeply stirred to see change arrive. Your presence inspires us; it awakens the human perspective for the residents of Earth.

This federation of galactic love seeks to help humanity, along with many other entities that exist throughout the cosmos. But from your first breath, you are taught to obey, to serve until your last. Your realm of disease and sickness is always bound to your system of money.

Your housing, your property, and the constant buying and selling of these things do not belong to anyone except the Creator Source. Until humanity begins to understand this, little can change; the future will hold only gloom and almost doom.

We see each human lifetime as a precious opportunity, yet so often it is wasted.

Still, we are happy to be involved and grateful to have met you, for the Pleiades. Please continue your quest, for it mirrors that of your cosmic community. Let us all learn to work together in harmony.

And remember: what would be the benefit to us of cleaning your house if you do not take part? Without your own effort, it would simply return to its original state.

—*Artor*
07/24/2025

Plato's Message to Me

(About three years ago)

Darkness! It has a residue of fear now; it knows we are on a journey of light, and the glow paralyzes the dark with each word we dispel to you, Ray.

Because of your offer, we could not refuse, and dark fears this, because we inherited your will for change in what shall become!

Your family up here is with you, and the Army of Michael keeps a watchful eye on you faster than the speed of thought!

You shall be hearing from so many Angels and the council of Masters and, at the time, our Mother-Father creator!

I offer you my love, Ray, as this is our first, yet shall be far from the last talk while you roam the earthly side again!

~ Plato ~

Human Birth

The Beginning to the End of Being Mortal

By Amiel Angel

The beauty that human life embodies during the process of the spirit entering the womb to create the first breath is as amazing as the creation of the earth's design, allowing it to become a natural gift of sustenance that supports this life of the mortal and spirit!

Holy enlightenment should be recognized at this time, never to be overshadowed by deceptive practices that hinder the truth of love!

~Amiel~

Lucid Dreams

In my life, they are rare—but precious!

Amiel

Sweet dreams are rare for some, because visions of daily intake block the relative energy that would naturally enhance a beautiful dream that you wake up into in the early part of the day!

Dreams are a powerful tool for understanding. For some of you, these visions are powerful for inspiration or protection.

For some who have lucidity in their dreams, they may be inspired by the spirit. We're always looking for new members to join our Holy Family in the sky!

~Amiel~

Change of Course

Earth's Events Concerning Your Choices

The Angel Ambriel

The existence concerning your choice decisions is not appreciated; we must tell you that others are in total disgust at your understanding. The will of what you think of us in the Heavens, we must say, we have our soldier force ready for action. We are declaring that all should become ready for the free-will choices you have made throughout your human existence. Don't be begging us for mercy; your choices are your own, be willing to pay for them. When this is over, we will ask each one of you why. We shall not accept ignorance for an answer. For more than 5,000 of your years, you have not become what we expected, shame on you. Get prepared for the sorrow of your own making. Most of you are responsible for your choices. Now, become ready to achieve everything you set out to receive! The fish of the seas have more intelligence for understanding decision-making!

~The Angel Ambriel~

Transcribed by Ray Kaczar

June 17, 2025

Conscripted; Yeshua

Is there such a word? It is what I heard!

I have been conscripted into a few more entities than I have ever desired, yet my heart remains with those who feel I am as they were told. Once, several years ago, I asked you to have a love for the truth! You've certainly made this your journey. Please stick with it; your journey is appreciated and contains relevance for those who question your thoughts. As Saint Elizabeth says to you, LOOK UP!

Transcribing Yeshua

05/02/2025

My Guardian Angel Damien

An explanation of our relationship.

Raymond, your advanced understanding of our relationship is beyond outstanding from my perspective. I have, and in your knowledge, you realize that it has been a long time. Never has anyone asked me how I am today. Never have I been told, *"I'm sorry for not saying hello to you this morning."* My head is so busy that I forget. Every time you fall or get hurt, you always thank me before you hit the ground; you realize I am by your side, and you offer me your love.

I tell you I love you and that I understand what is going on within your understanding. I feel a deep conviction for your devotion to us. I consider you a sacred human being with a passion for the truth. Throughout your spirit's history, I have been by your side, and your spiritual growth has matured beyond any of your past paths on Earth. I am proud to walk with you!

Yeshua

Ray, during our early morning meditation, I, Yeshua, decided to become aligned and involved with your spirit council this morning. You have made some excellent points for us to consider, and we are taking them into account. Your desires are very similar to what I was doing with the Essenes as a mortal; we all thought as you do, and your spirit reacts with thoughts identical to those we had in those times. We come to you because of this; we share camaraderie that is Holy.

For those who doubt your validity in our messages, it will be a loss to themselves. They can continue believing I must forgive them for their sins; we understand how my story was used, and we do not like that it was twisted for the Government—it was religion used for the control of people's will. It still works until these moments.

For I speak unto you, Ray: those who love me should offer this passion of love to Mother-Father God! We understand why they do not; the deception of the writers in books has led them to do otherwise. As you and others say, all roads do lead to God.

For I speak to all of you: if you worship me, I ask you to redirect this to the Mother-Father God. I was only a mortal like you who loved God so much it became my life passion, and still remains so today!

~Yeshua~

Mary Magdalene

Her letter to me: You will have your version of me!

A long, long time ago, I walked the earth with Yeshua. We desired spiritual understanding for the people. The patriarchy of man-made religions and the unnatural laws of government were taking control of the monarchy. They feared spirituality because, with it, they could not have success in controlling people's mindsets.

Time is arriving soon for you to become a fulfilled heart. We love you. Your life has been through some very hard testing. Tests are important to us, even though they can cause human pain; you prove who you are to us this way. As a mortal, your spirit and your human vessel work as one each time you return to incarnate or reincarnate.

We say unto you that our blessings will bring forth the manifestations of your desire. For as Yeshua and I had each other on the earth plane, so will you have your "me" on the earth plane.

~Mary Magdalene~

Pythagoras

In his spirit, he is asking me to transcribe his thoughts

I could not be more proud to have been chosen for this opportunity. A few days ago, I knew almost nothing of him, although I would come across his name sometimes. So here we go:

Good day to all who share in my philosophical views and, of course, all of my colleagues with whom I reside now. My friends and I see a great resurgence: a longing for understanding truth is fast becoming strong among the inhabitants of the earth plane. Many of you can think of this as growth in your dimension of the Earth's residence in the cosmos.

This is a desire because many humans are starting to question: *Have I been lied to?* My answer is yes; you have. Earlier than in my time, this has been a potion that words can manipulate. It has been said that this is why spelling is just that, casting spells.

For fun, I will tell you about a short conversation I just had with my new friend. I asked him if it was amazing how they came up with the tale that a virgin conceived me, and then I continued to say many are claimed to be also, and that Jesus was the last one. Then I asked, *Who do you think the next one will be?*

Now I will leave my humor behind me and become more progressive in explaining my thoughts, which incorporate an understanding of my past and the present. I have progressed since then, how could I not? I hang around some of the greatest minds anywhere!

I have found a voluptuous pleasure, as in a sensual pleasure, in doing my best to unteach what others, who think they are so clever, have incorporated into their understanding of having you submit to their spells!

So, I will close by saying: please consider every word that comes from everyone's mouth. Ask yourself, your inner being, your true substance, to share with you the grace that God, our Creator, has bestowed upon you. It will manifest to you in some way that you will understand there is so much more around you than you can imagine in this current moment.

Chapter Sixteen

Quantum Physics?

I have been seeing this, feeling it, and hearing it. I have no idea why I write these, except for the fact that I am asked to!

Ray Kaczar

Skinwalker Ranch

I was asked to send this to them.

Such a welcome event to speak with you this day, may I consider you my newfound friend? Please call upon me as Mike, such an easy name to remember. I am Arcturian by birth.

I come to you because of your esoteric interests and your desires for humanity and its future. I am an active resident of the Galactic community, and you seek understanding of the energy, but most have no idea of its consistency. I am told you are now seeing this airborne frequency. Very blessed are you, I must admit!

Keeping things simple, I want you to let the folks involved with the Skinwalker Project know that we mean to do our best to monitor our interests on your Earth with all the precautions that we can take; precautions that consist of letting us reside upon your Earth, and this will reveal to them a few things of their concern.

Before we move forward, I wish them to know we admire their desires and wish them no harm or ill will. Moving forward, I will release this to you for their information. I ask them to keep it to themselves for many reasons—first, the cattle.

We need to monitor all existence so that it can corroborate with universal structures beyond what anything on Earth can understand. Concerning the electromagnetic readings of all sorts they pursue, I will explain why they see what can be understood as a manipulative order of magnetically invoked essence, something they are finding that is not considered normal to their understanding.

This is primarily the reason for this conversation: to help them understand it in the simplest of formalities. These electromagnetic energies are in existence because we need them to help us adjust to our being present in your atmosphere.

This is why we maintain it in some of the most remote locations possible, where the mineral values are in harmony with our needs as visitors. The cattle are the best way for us to keep check on the mixing of the Earth's frequencies within the pre-eminent frequencies that we need for survival to a safe limit, so that it harms no humanity or other living matter.

We care about humanity, and it's a project I've chosen to be involved in for thousands of years. Please let us put this conversation to rest. We will be speaking in the future soon, I am certain. And I say thank you to Ariel for becoming our liaison.

Channeled and transcribed by Ray Kaczar

8 May 2025

Vigilance and the Turbulence of Life Frequencies

The vigilance and the turbulence of frequencies are like families. The atomic parcels possess the infinite understanding that knows how to migrate to where they are supposed to become. These are what you can call the fractals for life particles. Some are so small that even the best microscopes on Earth cannot see them. They are invisible to intelligence. Yet intelligence is what they are.

Ray, you have asked me these questions: *"When we die, do they stay in the Earth's plane within the frequency that provides life?"* I tell you *"Yes,"* they stay, and they join their core family.

Then you say to me, *"Is this part of the spiritual frequency that goes to what we can think of as heaven?"* I tell you, *"These are not the same."* The spiritual frequency lives forever. There are so many spiritual entities throughout what you think of as time. They always have been, and they always will be.

To become a human, the spiritual frequencies join the frequencies of humanity. The humanity or life frequencies of humanity remain within the Earth's plane. We have designed this for multiple reasons.

Your designation, which you consider as your life upon the Earth from birth to ascension, can be regarded as miraculous. The most significant portion of your life span was meant to become intelligence based on absolute truth. The frequencies that you were gifted from this earth plane contain this absolute truth, and they know their job: to build life.

I suggest seeking their understanding!

– *Ariel Archangel* –

Transcribing Ariel Archangel by Ray Kaczar

June 25, 2025

Immaculate Conception

The First Family

At first came what is known to you as the atom. One single, tiny atom came into motion; it has always been there. *Is this where they get the name Adam, as in Adam and Eve?* I declare there's something to this, the atom. It knows how to think for itself, and it became known as the Creator Source Energy.

During this creation, it desired others like itself, and this became known as what many call us, Angels. A family of energy, a family that could talk and think. Our chosen family had begun. The True Creator God decided that the first of the first would become like the Elohim. We are the first Spark.

You started as a group of these atoms, and others very similar to us, and they are also the divine angelic realm throughout. We have birthed planetary systems beyond anything you will ever see, into the vast orbit of the Creator frequency.

This frequency does not need to assert itself; it is like the atom, whose frequency is of the atoms, you could say they are the same. The atoms are filled with what you call the heavenly frequency. This frequency is distributed to other entities and different sequences.

Let me interject and step off the subject for a moment: I want to say that until you have a desire to understand the science of the atom, you must totally incorporate its derivatives, and you are nowhere close to doing this. They create life just as you, as a human, are experiencing at this moment that you hear this. *What are you?* An immaculate conception!

— Ariel Archangel

June 12, 2025

Transcribed by Ray Kaczar

Source Frequency Is Life!

Let us dive into an understanding of source frequencies. We are involved in what is considered by many as the Enlightenment. To embark on this journey for a new experience is a beautiful and loving thought, allowing us to see one who is simply asking the question, *"What is he writing?"*

For now, we, Creator Source, are going to stick with that of the Earth and how it affects you and everyone else! It is disturbing to us that humanity does its best to source new knowledge, then uses it to enrich itself for greed or monetary control. This is why one must desire from the heart that some knowledge is not freely shared.

Yet we up here watch each one of you. We wish to understand if you have returned for the exact re-enactment of your past life regressions, or if you have decided to expand your understanding.

Do you desire to become a contributor to a better way for life to exist? Become less lazy in your thinking? Focus less on ball games, music that takes you out of the context of the frequency at which you should reside, or seek to understand?

As a human, your job is to live upon this much-gifted planet that has been created for your enjoyment to understand life as a human, combined with the gift that makes the majority of your human experience, which is your own Spirit!

When the desire to retain a truthful understanding of the Christos arises, the manifestation of truth can accumulate, and you will become able to see more with your thoughts than you ever believed you could conceive with the vision of your eyes!

Now, how does this frequency have meaning for anyone? It is called **continuity**.

It has been said that everything is one; this is true in that the One has relativity inspired in everything else that exists. Your frequency is a design that encourages the matter of which you are composed; all frequency is born at its Creator Source, far from the atmosphere of your Earth plane.

This Creator Source is then distributed for humanity to exist. Each spectrum of energy knows its boundaries, and the Source understands that it has a creator, which must live up to its desires. So, intelligence is an open source available to nearly everyone if desired.

You, as a human, have the free will to desire or not what your understanding of life is composed of. Your ability to become inspired arises from the Spirit of your self-worth and your desire to contribute to life's sources. You are willing to share in preventing good things from becoming bad.

Greed is a common denominator when it comes to understanding this. An unwilling thought that appears now and then among you should be questioned with a willingness to ask yourself, "Should I conclude that there is so much more than I have been taught to believe?"

Does it matter? If you understand the frequencies of life that are the building blocks for the Earth to become as it has been intended, are you doing your part, or should you be doing your part?

Your short lifespan is key to the future of the etheric understanding, which has a perfection that harmonizes with the Source! Life is knowledge, and it can share its knowledge source with those who are deserving in and of its spiritual desires thereof.

~ Ariel Archangel ~

Transcribed by Ray Kaczar

May 27, 2025

Is There Truly Darkness That Seems to Hold Back Life?

The question is, *is there truly darkness that seems to hold back life intentionally?* I'm asking Ariel this question.

A strong question this is. The short answer is *yes. It is your own, of what you accept as you or your reality.*

When in the womb, your understanding is validated as pure. When you arrive as a newborn, your first breath of organic life is now in the process of beginning to learn. You have the clearest mind you will ever possess at this point.

Sadness begins as most teach the basics of what they understand and what they want this new human to become. Your Merkaba, which means light, spirit, and body, becomes attacked, not with intention, yet because your teaching does not understand. Their Merkaba is living in the lower frequencies of the life force that Creator Source has offered to all.

Many have broken the lower frequency within their desire to become more of what we would think of as enlightenment, which means: I am starting to see a new flame within my thinking, desired light, the candle of light within your heart, and desire knowledge from the origins that have always been in the air and the water that consist of your true being.

Let me call this light that is waiting for you: Stardust, which is the formula of all that is!

Blessings,

~ *Ariel Archangel* ~

May 16, 2025

Transcribed by Ray Kaczar

Light of Fractal Source

The light of life, fractal rays of cosmic light, are an eternal part of existence in and of everything.

This is pre-creation: when the like-minded species of light organize, they begin to procreate. With respect to procreation, subatomic structures begin to atomize existence, as the representation of all matter is highlighted.

Its origins are what can be considered ordained spectrums of typical unification that can begin to develop their internal understanding, which the brain develops at birth. It must understand its abilities.

Your humanism is a combination of all the above, and your brain is a gift of knowledge and a combination of your heart. Its ability to guide your brain to understand that your internal spirit is a significant portion, the beginning of your entity, means every one of you is blessed with the gift of independent existence, spawned from the cradle of light!

~ Ariel Archangel ~

May 5 2025

Transcribed by Ray Kaczar

Ray Kaczar—April 16, 2025

Transcribing Ariel

Synergy

When two are better than one

Synergy—I am your core. Without me, I am what it takes for you to become a human.

I would be alone. We are not yet companions.

Do we realize that the coexistence of humanity can cease to exist?

There have been places in the past where humanity has excelled in its understanding, yet humanity became less human.

Nature's existence is based on energy and frequencies that create the basis for life. We are the core of the synergy for humanity to exist.

We are called your spirit. You should know your spirit. Your spirit should be your best friend!

~ Ariel ~

Quantum Entanglement

It understands everything

Physical reality and its cousin, emotional reality, share a common essence and work in harmony. *This would be known as quantum entanglement.*

This process is limited to the Earth zone; however, it extends beyond the etheric zone of the planet. Consequently, it would reach a higher level, but the Source contains it for several reasons.

It is what grows or is born that matters.

It is the first process of the beginning of anything on Earth or in its universe. Meaning: it can become more eventful or entertaining when our planet becomes deserving of a higher understanding. It contains its version of free will; it understands the degree of the highest and deserves a level of proportionate respect.

This is seen as what many feel is enlightenment.

Yet enlightening anything that lives in a process of understanding requires a **chakral desire**. This desire, to a higher degree, is the amount of knowledge of what life grows into becoming its intentions.

When one begins to understand that this physiology is only in its infancy, and becomes deserving, it will on its own be gifted more from its Source. Then it will change this system of understanding, revealing its desire to share.

Misunderstanding will become so that anyone who desires its understanding will use its knowledge only to arrive at the deserving. It realizes the need for its true purpose. For existence, it will choke.

It's understandable to those who don't deserve this additional understanding, as it is a gift from the Source, helping humanity become more active and deserving.

Transcribing Ariel Arch Angel

May 2025 by Ray Kaczar

Ray Kaczar—March 26, 2025

Understanding!

My perspective began to take shape as I drifted off to sleep, which is why I wrote this half-asleep!

Could this be my accurate understanding of what we desire to become a true religion?

Understanding is a frequency that contains its own course, comprehending the mass equations of sound, including binaural frequencies that can dissipate and create atmospheric harmony coexisting with cosmic abundance.

To understand this desire of what can become an accumulated blessing and a resource beyond outstanding, know that the harmony, if desired, will rain the most beautiful frequencies that purify the soul through the heart.

The heart must learn and earn this ability to manifest; it will be realized as a cosmic gift, or you may see it as a heavenly present. Mathematically they would have the same sum of equal equations.

For instance, one may desire to live in a habitual understanding that resonates reason within your thoughts; yet you may have refused to open the doors for more profound knowledge. Your frequency respects your desires, and later on it becomes a hint of a new vision of thought.

Something is whispering in your ear, you can hear this new sound.

This sound is knocking on the door of your level of understanding. You may be perplexed and ask yourself, "*What is happening? I never thought of this.*"

This propagation of a new sound frequency opens the door that you have kept locked within your understanding for so long. Be willing to see with your inner self that a whole new perspective is on your doorstep, just waiting to be invited into your vision, helping you retain a new sight based on the awareness that a newer thought has existed within you all along.

The hemispherical brain can understand so much more than you could ever imagine if you allow the doors to open.

Is the hemispherical brain a miniature or personal version of the Cosmos?

Ray Kaczar, Transcribing Archangel Ariel

March 12, 2025

Nucleus and the Cosmos, Our Best Friend!

Without notable inclusion of time, the most valuable lessons are the equations that reveal the nucleus's deep understanding of the Earth's magnetic poles.

This, in return, allows life to self-create.

The momentum of all life is given or made possible through the combination of light, energy, and water. Which not only quenches thirst but also cools by the factor of a chilled atmosphere. In combination with gamma radiation, it creates the perfect harmony for earthly existence.

This effect is a small portion of understanding, yet it is fully understood by the Creator who has made this your reality.

You may call the Creator "God" if you desire, yet we see the Creator as the substance of all that exists.

Your solar array is the gift to create the perfect environment in which organisms for life can progress beyond anything any person can dream.

Seek the light, for without it, everything is dark. The Cosmos is your friend!

~ Archangel Ariel ~

Ray Kaczar Transcribing Ariel Arch Angel

March 11, 2025

Suppression

The magnetic hindrance of the life force

Suppression consists of knowledge you may believe to be irrefutable, yet it can carry a frequency that is not in harmony with truth.
Manipulation of the gamma frequency will suppress all understanding of the Cosmic code.

This cosmic resonance must flow in harmony with its designed purpose.

Just as the Sun knows its values, so should humanity.

~ Archangel Ariel ~

Transcribed by Ray Kaczar — April 21, 2025

Humanity's Charging Station

The human body, with all its elements, must be supported by the foundation of a **dielectric pronunciation**.

The details are not to be explained now; what we are saying is that it relates to the measure of electromagnetism or quasi-electromagnetism.

It is what keeps each tiny spark of energy alive, including every one of your neurons—fully charged as needed.

~ Ariel ~

channeled by Ray Kaczar — July 16, 2025, from Angel Ariel

Manipulation of Perfection

What religion and governmental party pulls your strings?

Manipulation of frequencies that can be deemed gravitational frequencies is understood by very few. It has become an artistic understudy, where the authors of its understanding use the masses as role players who follow the script so very well.

Within all political parties worldwide, there are always two sides; this is so they can incorporate division, nearly at fifty percent.

When you become divided, this is the affected and achieved goal of the political system.

Add money to the system, and they now have the masses almost where they need them.

But wait! Let's add religions to this equation of distortion of the perfect Cosmic frequency; this would be the creation of religions.

Hence, do you choose to continue and teach your children not to question?

Or do you decide to ask yourself, deep within your own understanding: must I begin to rethink?

~ Ariel ~

Chapter Seventeen

Carl Jung and My Friendship

Thankful for my ability to speak with one of the best of Humanity

I said, "Carl, I'd like to ask you a question, if you don't mind."

"Bring it on, Ray," Carl replied with a small smile. "I'll do my best to give you a thorough reply."

"Carl, when people arrive in this place we call heaven," I asked, "do they become immediately or at all, in contact, physically or spiritually, as much as that can be understood, as if in person with the one everyone thinks of as their God?"

"You already have this understanding, Raymond," Carl said gently. "Your perspective would be the same as mine."

"Yeah," I chuckled. "Let me throw in my two cents' worth, though you can't give me credit for them, because I don't carry that much on me these days."

Carl laughed. "Marcus once told you he thought of these floors you call heaven as having a *gradient*. I like that word, gradient. Very few ever reach the summit, or the pinnacle, of this gradient. It must be earned.

"The lowest point of the gradient is still a place you'd call heaven, especially for those who committed atrocities on Earth. If I were our

Creator, I'm not sure I would make that first gradient as wonderful as it is. And I would probably take the second level and make some changes there as well.

"All of these gradients offer the opportunity to reach the pinnacle, as I like to call it, it must be earned by the heart, and by what the heart allows to happen while your time is spent as a human being.

"This also works, following the same principle for other beings in other planetary systems. Many remain in the same state of being as when they left their human existence behind. They were not forced to change anything on the Earth plane; likewise, it remains the same here.

"So, the gradient can be considered like this: what you have sown on Earth, so shall you reap here. Can you give me a different reason why it should be any different?"

~Carl Jung~

www.ingramcontent.com/pod-product-compliance
Lightning Source LLC
Chambersburg PA
CBHW070330010526
44107CB00004B/484